LIFE IS ABOUT DECISION LIFE IS ABOUT LOVE

BLESSING BESS OTOBO

To Kitty Smith
From Bess Otobo
B.Otobo
6/10/22
Thank you!

LIFE IS ABOUT DECISION: LIFE IS ABOUT LOVE

IS

DEDICATED TO YOU

CONTENTS

QUESTION:

Are you tired and weary that your effort to find satisfaction in life is unfruitful? Do you go to bed feeling sad and empty, defeated and discouraged? Have you asked yourself, "What am I doing wrong, and what can I do differently?" Have you asked the questions; "Why do other people seem to have it all and I don't?" So if the answer to any of these questions is a yes, please look no further because the answer to your questions lies within you.

WHAT IS THE SECRET TO LIFE

❖❖❖❖❖❖

What do you think is the secret of life success? The Secrets that could likely catapult you from the lowest point of awareness to a level of unimaginable heights. The secret that is perhaps the source of your everyday experience and one for which you may not be aware. What is this secret, or the key to happiness most people have searched for or wondered about?

I too have had these exact questions in my head several times and have wondered what the secret is? Why the feeling of discouragement? Why the dissatisfaction in life? What is wrong with me? As Socrates once said, "the unexamined life is not worth living." So, I began re-examining how things have been laid out in my life and to my amazement, I saw what was wrong.

The secret like the most essential element of life is very facile, and as a matter of fact, it's all around you. If you look at your surroundings, whether you are seating or standing, you will notice various objects around you.

Every inanimate object you observe is a derivative of this secret, meaning they originate from this secret. Subjectively, some objects are beautiful and some are not; but the fact is there are objects all around you.

I know you are wondering right now what this author is talking about. I will come to that later, but first, I will like you to take a deep breath and exhale. If you have done that, I will like you to write down on a piece of paper what you think is the most essential element of life; what do you think is the most important thing in life? If you wrote, "air" as your primary source of life, you are absolutely correct. The most vital source of life is the air we breathe. Without air, there would be no evidence of life, yet some people may not be aware of this aspect of their lives or value it until perhaps something traumatic happens.

In a very practical way, without the oxygen in the atmosphere there would be no life. Think about this; why is it that air is so important yet kept in the open space? Why is this? The reason air is abundant and in the open space is so that we would know that the creator of all living things, including man is real and that His riches are abundant to all. Why would any person give life so abundantly without restriction; unless the person is generous?

And he is generous because he knows air comes from a place of abundance and fills every space? Isn't it amazing that the creator of heaven and earth is inexhaustible? Imagine that, and the creator gives everything so generously. Some rich men and women who are generous are so because they believe the saying; "the earth is the Lord's and the fullness thereof." They know that life is full of abundant blessings, and what they sow, they will also reap.

This also applies to the creator of our souls. God gave man breath, the very source of life because it is abundantly stored up. If the air is given to man generously; is anything limited? No. If the most essential thing in life like air is free, can you imagine what else is free? My point is that it came from a place of plenty.

If the air we breathe weren't abundantly stored up, it would be unimaginable for anyone to survive especially in the way humans are selfish with the perishable things of nature. Honestly, if air were for sale, the people who could afford it would be those who have the money to buy it. But thank God, air is not for sale otherwise those who perceived themselves as poor would be deprived of it. So if the air we breathe is freely given, is there anything that is not freely given? Everything is freely given.

The secret to life that many of us are not aware of is also freely given. The air we breathe is kept in the open so that every living being on earth would know the answer to the greatest puzzle called life; that everything is just as effortless as the air. If only we can trust that everything imaginable is attainable because it has already been given freely. If the most precious thing in man's life is the air he breathes which sustains his life, then everything else is secondary. If you think otherwise, perhaps you may need to take an inventory of what you define as important. Air like this secret is the very foundation of your life experience, the first principle of your existence.

And like every significant factor in life that is free, people become careless with it and misuse it because it was freely given. Fortunately, some who know that what is given freely can also be freely taken away have guarded their gifts with diligence. When we misuse what has been given freely without knowing its importance, we violate the true principle that works for us. Air is an important element, yet we take it for granted by polluting the atmosphere with chemicals that are potentially harmful to our lungs. Another aspect of life that is essential to all living beings is water. Water is vital to life because it has the essence of life in it.

Water is made up of two molecules of oxygen, and one of the elements is air or energy. What this means is that air is an essential component of life. When the O in H_2O is removed, you are in essence taking out the vital part from it, and nitrogen alone cannot sustain life. Therefore, oxygen is required in order to have life in water. Invariably what I am trying to illustrate is that virtually every life-sustaining element is comprised of the most important essence of life, which is air. Take away the air from the food that you eat, and you have no life-sustaining substance in it.

As important as the air you breathe, so also is an element that I shall be revealing to you. The only difference is that some people are not entirely aware of it and have no prior knowledge of its importance to their existence or its effect on their physiological and psychological well-being.

But as you read further, you will realize that like water, which is used in formulating so many things that you use, so also is this secret absolute in conjuring everything seen around you.

As the types of food you eat can nourish your body, so is this secret. It can mandate and determine your future and everything that happens in it.

If you eat healthy food, you will maintain a healthy body, but if you continue eating unhealthy food, your body will adjust to your eating habit in a negative way.

The secret of life is necessary to the essence of who you are and equally important are the three elements mentioned before; which are water, air, and food. I know you are wondering right now, how do air and water correlate to the secret of life? I would say, view them according to their importance.

The air you breathe is crucial to your survival and a vital source of energy for your daily strength. Before I reveal what this secret is, I would like you to try an exercise. Close your eyes and visualize yourself in a place you've always wanted to be or with someone you've always wanted to be with. Now be aware that the emotions you attach to this image will produce a response or a feeling. Continue this exercise for five to ten minutes. Try not to entertain any other thoughts. See yourself in this place or with the person you've visualized. Try visualizing this image without too much effort. Just picture this image and leave it suspended.

When you entertain this presence for a number of times every day, you find out that this image is what you regularly see, and its essence is what you feel. If you practice it for a long time, it becomes a force that moves you towards the truth of it.

The reality of what you've pictured becomes if you don't negate it with doubt or fear. If you visualized doing something like being with a loved one, whether he/she is with you physically or not, you would feel the essence of the thing or your loved one with you. That is, depending on what emotion you attach to the image you hold in your mind, you will receive the same response. The response or feeling you get is the effect of your thought. I think by now you have an idea what the secret is.

The one element that controls you and your environment is your thoughts upon your mind. The way you measure your mind controls your experiences. The most powerful and yet simple weapon given to man by God, the Creator of our BEING is our THOUGHTS. It is your mind that was used in conjuring the image I asked you to conceptualize. It was your thought that formed the matrix of the presence you felt, the presence of your loved ones residing in you, and the things you would like to have.

Your thought is a tool (like the air you breathe) that creates everything around you. If your thought is not creating a reality for you, somebody else's thought is, which means your thought has taken a passive role. I would like you to know that everything around you was and is created by your thought or someone else's thought.

And remember wherever you go, you cover the distance first by thinking it through or someone thinking it through for you.

The mystery which was hidden from men generation to generation; has been revealed to men by the Spirit, (the essence of life), is the power that lies in the images of his thought. This revelation is only perceived with knowledge, without knowledge, there would be no insight to know that your beliefs are paramount to what happens to you in life.

In the book of Colossians, 1:25-26, Prophet Paul in his letters to the church, wrote. "The mystery which has been hidden from ages and from generations has been revealed to His saints." This secret is the fulfillment of God's words to those who believe in His son: the truth of life.

The mystery that has been revealed is the knowledge that when you believe in the word of God, the truth of his thoughts, the picture of what you want in your mind becomes as you believe it. Thoughts are life, and they create things. As Christ also said, "The words which He gave to you are spirit and are life." The truth is that the force or spirit will move you to what you have thought. Your thought is your power to create, and it has been given to you freely.

It is the key to unlocking all the blessings of God in your life. Your faith in the truth of your thoughts or words brings about the revelation or manifestation of what you've imagined.

God created everything in the universe with His truth. You as his creation have the same power available to you because that which God had from the beginning was impressed upon you before you were born. All the right things God had imagined before you were created can only materialize through you, through your thinking when you give it a chance to manifest. This is accomplished, as you believe in the truth of the goodness in you. God or the Creator of your soul is freedom expressed, to do all things when its truth in you is obeyed. God is a spirit or the life of man. And the man can live life harmoniously when he effortlessly submits to what is good in him. It is through the truth within you that you can reach God your Creator.

Unfortunately, many people don't believe in who they are and have veered off onto the wrong path, because of cultural and traditional conditioning. How to get back to the right course with God is a worthy question that will get a response.

In Mathew Chapter 7:7, The Lord said; "Ask, and it will be given to you; seek, and you will find; knock, and it will be opened to you."

Getting back to the right path with God is achievable. When you let go of the old pattern of thinking that held you captive and bound; the idle pleasures that are unproductive, (although some are productive, but not in your best interest) then you can be free to exercise what is good in you.

Many people are bound by culture, false religious beliefs, drug addiction, sex addiction, addiction to worldly pleasures and unhealthy thought patterns that have kept them bound. But they can still be set free and feel liberated again when they become aware of what has bound them in the first place.

When you become aware that your thoughts are the catalyst to things happening to you, and you want to be set free, you will do what is necessary to release yourself from what has kept you confined. Interestingly, many do not believe in the rebirth of the mind and the heart, or being born again. But unless one is reborn spiritually and intellectually, one cannot experience the freedom of averages; that is, freedom of what is right in everything. It is by psychological rebirth that the old self is loosened, and a new self, emerges.

When you believe in the truth of what you really want for yourself, you will definitely let go of what is not true for you, and when you do so, you become renewed intellectually and physiologically. The saints according to Apostle Paul are the believers of the word of God or the truth of life. The purpose of believers in Christ is to be the conduit through which the goodness of God is distributed on the earth.

Those who do what is right according to the righteousness in them are saints, (figuratively, because they obey the word of their creator) - the Godly scriptures which are the fabric of their being. Each time you believe in what is true of you, you lose the old pattern of thinking that negates your being.

Your subconscious mind is the foundation of your life's riches and blessings. Its principle is always positively charged and runs non-stop. The secret is that your thought is what unleashes the blessings in you, and for others. As you impress upon your mind what you want for yourself, it will become a reality since its principle is always active. Every time you think a thought, based on its laws, it becomes as real as you've thought it.

As quoted in Mathew 18:18 "Truly I say to you, whatever you shall bind on earth shall be bound in heaven: and whatever you shall loose on earth shall be loosed in heaven."

So each time you affirm that which you are thinking, it becomes. You are a law onto yourself. Your thought is the script of your life and the weapon given to you by your Creator to unlock all the blessings in the universe. As you write on the table of your mind, so it is in your body. The reality becomes that which you want. Your thought is the ready writer that you can use to bind on earth as it is done in heaven.

The object around you that I asked you to look at or the image I asked you to perceive consciously is the manifestation of what you've thought; the expression of what those who produced the objects wanted.

Your thought is the secret that can change your perception of what happens to you from now on. You have the power to change the view and the image that you've scripted into your subconscious mind. The key is releasing the old beliefs that have held you captive and believing the new image of what you want to happen in your life. You do that subtly, by focusing on what you wish to happen in your life; the new you. How it comes to being is not your concern, but the concern of the essence of it. Your business is to write down how you want your life to be; your vision or your dream and believe in it. How it happens is the business of the Creator.

When you believe in the rightness, so shall it be, when you think wrong, it will be. So, in essence, the images you are projecting are the hindrance or blessings in your life. If you perceive life experiences as sad, that's what you feel.

Then again, you change your perception and see life experience as joyous; that's exactly how you will feel because you have been entertaining thoughts of joy or forces of effortless submission to what is good. I will give you an example.

Let's say you pick up a bag of seeds, any kind of seed, and then you scatter the seeds on any soil. It could be your backyard garden, a garden with cow manure or a chemically infested ground. As long as that land is fertile and healthy, every seed sown on that soil will grow. The potential of the seed is already in it, and depending on the type of seed or soil, the seed would germinate and grow according to what the seed is.

Your thoughts are like seeds that have a life force, and though the foundation on which it lies may be poisoned by negative emotions and thus becomes a hindrance to you, you can change that. The awareness that you want a change within you alters the foundation of your thoughts completely and allows you the opportunity to think good and new thoughts. The power thus lies with he who plants the seed.

What seed have you been planting and what ground has it been planted on? Irrespective of what kind of seed that was planted, it will grow according to its kind.

A hypothetical explanation is in reference to the way people feel about certain diseases, for example, cancer. Let's say Mr. Tommy was diagnosed by a doctor and given three months to live. Mr. Tommy went home believing in the truth of his death that he would be dead in three months. In reality, Tommy will not make it to three months because based on the principle of his thoughts; the truth of his estimated date of death will be realized sooner. What he has believed is what is going to materialize for him.

The doctor may have confirmed that he has cancer and will die in three months. Tommy can still gain additional months and even years to live if he continuously sees and believes in the essence of perfect health. The truth of perfect health which already exists in him will become his new experience as he continues to think perfect health through the one healing power in him. The reason his health may deteriorate is based on his previous thought process or his beliefs. Belief is something that you acknowledged as fact, whether consciously or unconsciously. Your thought is your belief.

If Tommy has been given weeks to live and then he dies as predicted, it is because he has unconsciously projected the thought of illness in his mind that nothing else is visible but the truth of the cancer image in his mind. "I have cancer," he thinks. The essence of what he believes has become all that he sees and felt in his consciousness. And because they are his beliefs it became the reality of what the doctor has confirmed.

Tommy may have planted in his mind the thought of fear, the emotion of having deadly cancer. The ideas of imperfect health which fueled the truth of cancer cells in his body. Tommy has without knowing ceased believing in the truth of his health, but rather believed in the negation of health, which is his sickness. The cancer cells can and will leave his body when he changes his mental picture of the illness and his feelings about it and believes in the truth of perfect health. Health is the whole; sickness is a variation of what is not.

When Tommy stopped thinking of his perfect health, he discontinued living right and as such has disconnected the flow of pure life from the fact of his health. When he begins to change his mental picture to something other than his illness and starts to speak it out, he will experience and feel different.

When you want to get rid of fear of sickness or fear of death, read Revelation 12:11, " they overcame him (fear of diseases) by the word of their testimony. Also, read James 4:7, which says; "Submit your thoughts to God, resist the devil, and he will flee from you."

When you submit to God; the life principle in you, means you resist the thought of sickness, and as you focus on feeling good, the sickness will flee. Choose a different thought about the good and believe the truth that you can be healed.

Galatians Chapter 3:13, also puts it in clear perspective about what is already true for a person who believes in the power of Christ's redemption. Christ has redeemed us from the curse of the law; which means redeemed from anything that may entangle us to believe differently about the pure goodness that is in us. When you believe in the reality of Christ that is you, the spirit of righteousness and wholeness that exists even before you were born, you will overcome the thought of sickness. And especially when you keep affirming your health you are giving the testimony of what is true. Every action a person has ever taken in his life is faith and only in faith can one change the course of his health. Every human life is faith in truth.

Every thought or action that a person has ever conceived or taken is faith. "Seed time and harvest time," every thought like seed takes root and will manifest. Some thought processes or beliefs are subtle, but when you obey its rightness in you, you are obeying the commandments of God. Believing in the rightness of God can be felt as joy, peace, and love.

So also is believing in the false concepts of what others have projected to you, is also what you experience as daily frustrations of dealing with people you come in contact with.

The truth of your mental cultivation and response to external behavior or attitudes directed at you is a path to your progressive living or the failure in your daily activities. The images you perceive in your mind are important as the life in you, because, like the air, the images within you are life forces that are effortlessly present when you conceive of them. The thought-image you imagine has life and power in it to make it a reality.

The secret is to let the thought in your mind be the picture of good and for you to submit to its manifestation just as freely as the air you breathe effortlessly, because the Creator who formed you, fashioned you with what is effortlessly good.

You don't want to negate the intentions of good with negative thoughts because based on the ideas that created you, what you allow into your mind will be. It is like fire; whatever you place on it will burn because of the nature of fire. When you place something on fire, it affects the vessel placed on it. You have a life because of the air in your lungs, and when the air is not circulating correctly, you will eventually die from a lack of oxygen. You are a thinking man because of your mind. Without your mind, you are the beast that cannot think. The natural principle of air as a life force is the same with your thinking mind. The thoughts in your mind are active and when they are impressed upon with directions, the truth of what is impressed on the mind becomes your reality. This time, whether you speak it or not, it will still be because the force will compel you to act its truth.

There is life in you when the thoughts in your mind are positive and proactive. That is; you are vibrant when your mind dwells on and entertains what is lovely and good. When you stop thinking right, you disconnect the issue of what is life and good from the source of the creator in you. To live the life you want, you have to conceive a picture of how you wish to live. You must insist upon mentally seeing yourself surrounded by things and conditions as you wish them to be.

Your thought is creative. You might not be able to bring back your loved ones with your thoughts; but you can change the way you feel about them by the way you think of them; because they are always with you, whether you know it or see them or not. You have the power to feel love and live in the love of what their lives meant to you. This is where your power lies; the key to making a difference in how you feel about your loved ones.

Make sure the images you have about them is of peace, joy and all that is lovely. This is the only way you can harmoniously bond with your loved ones and rejoice in the life they've lived. Remember that you were conceived from the image of God; His imagination, thus His character, His rightness.

If God did not imagine you in goodness, you would not be formed. God created you because you are good; therefore, you should not destroy what is good by thinking negatively about yourself or others. If you have ever felt frustrated or hurt by the feeling of failure, there is a reason for it; and the reason is the way you use your thoughts in relation to your self and the situation.

Your frustrations and hurt were created by your thoughts and the way you were reacting to circumstances. According to the book of Genesis, 1:1; God created the world by speaking the substance of what He wanted into being.

He said, "Let there be light, and there was light." God spoke the word. The word, which is life, and the life, which is God, became what the creator had conceived in his mind. God is the good he created; God's life is a man; the word manifested: God created man in his image.

If the word, which dwells in His believers is life, what then is the life? Life is the word of God represented and the Creator within His believers.

Without the life-giving force or the image of the creator, the life in man, there would be no man. Without you thinking right, there will be no manifestation of what is right in you.

The very essence of water is the air, without the air in water, water is just hydrogen and other elements that aren't life sustaining. The blood in our veins is mixed with water and oxygen. Without oxygen and water in our blood, the very essence of life that is in man would not be. Isn't it ironic that the very essence of life has been given to us freely as a gift? When we breathe, the lungs automatically filter the impurities from the air we breathe in. We should do likewise, by dwelling on the thoughts that edify the mind, soul, and body. If you recall when I asked you to imagine a picture of a person that made you feel good,

I bet you experienced a sense of calm and peace; a feeling that produced confidence in you and made you believe in its reality. What you actually experienced was your thought or beliefs in images, which is everything I have been trying to say.

Your idea became real in you as you experienced the effects, which can be peace and calm, or fear and doubt. When you focus on a thought, on a concept or on a person you want to be with, you experience a sense of oneness with that individual; an emotional bond with that person.

The reason for such feeling is because the concept of that individual originated from your thought, your imagination of that person and then it became real in your mind. Whatever awareness you experienced when you think, such as a feeling, is the essence of your thought. Whatever object or substance you focus your thought on takes root and force and becomes your new self. Therefore, you should think good thoughts, because your thoughts are the road map that determine how you live and communicate.

Your thought is the tapestry of your existence, without your thoughts, like the air or the water you drink to stay alive, you are nothing and can't function. Have you pictured yourself without your faculties? What would become of you without it? It is impossible to be human without any perception of the self or the awareness of what you are.

The emotion behind your thought is what determines what becomes of your daily experiences. There is life in your thoughts, the concept that inhabits your mind. Your thinking is the seed of life. You plant it every day from the moment you wake up till the moment you fall asleep. Sometimes we make mistakes by the decisions we make. If the decisions that you've made have caused you pain, you can change it by realizing where your thoughts veered.

Some mistakes can be disastrous and may not be reversed, but if you recognize the mistake you made, you can correct some of it by speaking the opposite of what is currently present. Speak the truth of what you want. "The Lord sent his word and healed them."

YOUR THOUGHT AS A SEED

The word seed has different symbolic meaning, and in a logical sense, a seed is something that is planted in the soil in order for it to germinate into its kind. Your thought as a seed symbolizes different things and meaning.

In the analytical and practical sense, your thought is the way you think and see things; the patterns of accepting things, images that filter through your visual senses and sound effects that you can hear. Seed symbolically illustrates in the simplest fashion the manifold of man's existence or the word, the thought form.

The seed or the word of God is a separate life substance that dwells in man. Whenever the word, 'seed' is used, it demonstrates the power of the seed existing as an independent force. Like the thought form of man, the seed is a life force that operates as its principle dictates, but man has the ultimate power to control the seed or else the seed controls him.

If you are not in charge of your thoughts, your thoughts will control you, prompting you to do like the life force of the thoughts dictate.

The power lies in knowing that the seed has been given to you to use only for your benefit, by believing in it, that is, the truth of the seed. Man, as created by God, can channel the course of his life in every direction he wants it to go that is beneficial. A thought image gives way to emotions after the idea has been conceived, spoken or reacted to.

When words are spoken, what echoes out is the air that then gives off sounds that convey meanings through the image of what was communicated. Your thought like your breath is necessary because it is spirit and life. Your thought is your life in essence, and every generation of man is a regeneration of what came before by their thinking pattern. The key is that the thinking can be altered and changed by the power which is in you.

Every generation of man is distinctive by the way they think. Your thought propels your destiny, thus your future. Therefore, if you are weary and dissatisfied with your life, it is because you are not thinking the right thoughts. When you begin to change the way you think and react to events you come in contact with, your experiences of life will be different.

THOUGHTS AS THE AIR

※※※※※

I want to clarify this point, when I said 'thought' as the air, I meant in their parallel. Your thought is never the air that you breathe although it is comparable to the natural and spiritual symbol of it. How is this possible, you would say? How can the thoughts of man be the air he breathes? As a correlation; a man's thoughts relate to the air he breathes in its effortless essence.

Your thought is not the air, but it is also like the air you breathe in the sense that it is freely given to you, and it is a vital force of life in you. Your thoughts correlate to the air you breathe on its function.

In Genesis, Chapter 1:1, the word reads: "In the beginning, God created the heavens and the earth. The earth was on the face of the deep. And the Spirit of God was hovering over the face of the waters and God said, "Let there be light, and there was light. God saw the light, and it was good, and God divided the light from the darkness." The unseen element that hovers over the face of the water in the air, and in that air is the ether, the life-giving spirit. Your thought like the air hovers in your mind, impressing upon your mind mental images. Air, as we know is invisible in our visual world, yet in it is a vital element that sustains life. The ether, which is in the essence of air, was hovering over the deep water.

"The thought of God," according to Genesis 1:1, is, in essence " the spirit that was hovering over the face of the waters." In correlating this analogy to your thought, like the air that is hovering over the deep, your thoughts hover over your subconscious mind freely in the air over the deep. Your belief is activated when you emotionalize what you are thinking and when it is spoken out as God did ("And God said, let there be light, and there was light") it will manifest from the dark to the light, giving a sound that conveys meaning.

One other example is this, if you've been to the sea, one of the invisible life forces that hover over the face of the sea is the effortless air. We feel it when it blows across our face, but we cannot see it. Like your thought, you don't see it, but its force is hovering over your mind, the deep sea.

The light is man's awareness and understanding of what he has conceived, thought out or programmed in his mind in reference to when God said; "let there be light." You are aware of the impact of your ideas through your life experiences and your feelings. Your feelings are your responses to your thoughts.

The light that was good is impacted on man's mind consciously as he understands the meaning of his thoughts and how they relate to his reality. The light was separated from darkness, like intelligence from ignorance, from what was not known to what is known and felt. The darkness represents the mindset prior to conceiving thoughts that caused understanding or brought forth meaning to what was mentally conceived and realized.

When God spoke the word of light, His preconceived image went forth by faith to establish and to become what was designed. As a representation of God, you can pronounce or speak the thought image out for the word to be or act out the good that you've conceived mentally.

The original word that was spoken, the light that was pronounced came true from the breath of God. He spoke His word, which was through the air in you and in it His image was released out of his mind to yours. Air gives a sound when spoken, and this sound is that which was formulated, the pictures of the good things to come.

When you talk, if there is no sound, there is no meaning, as such there is no light (intelligence) or comprehension (understanding).

This also works the same way when you don't do what is necessary to fulfill the right image about yourself; in this sense, it will not be realized because you did nothing.

The spoken word also parallels the written word or action taken toward what was preconceived. If a person does not understand a word spoken, two things happened; the word was not audible and the sound did not register. The sound expressed is impressed upon the individual by images which then convert to meaning. Images are really words in essence, and they can only materialize when that which is in them is presented either as spoken language or action of some sort.

It doesn't matter what word or thought was used, what matters is that as long as the words are spoken or acted out, it will by its principle of rightness become what was intended. Air is the life we breathe, and this life is the word of God, his good idea for man.

The essence of your heavenly thoughts or God's word is the foundation of your existence, the decision to make that foundation a place you want to live in.

Make a right decision about what you conceptualize by carefully choosing your thoughts. The truth is in you, and all that is required of you is to live it as it has been designated, holy and pure.

When you do that, your freedom and blessing are sure because they had already begun in the beginning when God created you with his DNA. The truth is, every good image that you conceive mentally is already in you. Life is good, life is God, and God is His word; His word is the life in you that is good.

You are the real thought of God, and you are a gift to yourself to treasure. Your responsibility is how to protect yourself, the way it was from the beginning; whole, because you are pure. We were formed in His image. He breathed the breath of life. Though God is present within man, it is through man's thought that He can entertain any goodness in relation to what is His purpose in life for you. God is separate from mans' thought, but in no way apart from it.

God is present where man is because His image, His thought is man's essence of being. Man is not God, even though God's thought is an image called man. God is separate, but always present. God is ever present in person, within man and all around and through man's thinking.

As you can see, man's thought is pretty much a vital life source. As an intelligent person, I presume you will not deliberately sit in an environment that is polluted and inhale impurities in the atmosphere.

Although, these days that seems to be the case with the situation we find ourselves because some environments are polluted. What happens is that you will stay away from a polluted area so you don't inhale the dust and become sick. Your thought to stay away from a polluted area is your weapon of prevention. The weapon to do something about the situation involving your safety is the power given to you.

The impurities or pollution parallels your concept of what is false or the dissatisfaction you've experience with your life. When your thought of life is faulty, that is a sign that you are not doing what is right in regards to your thinking. Your power is to think the opposite of the negative that you are feeling; because that is the only way you can change the situation for your good. You think of good things when you want to feel good. When you change the ways you view yourself and replace it with new pictures of what you wish to see; things will begin to look different in your life and you will see the difference.

The more enthusiasm and faith that you are able to put into the picture you have in your mind, the quicker it will come into visible form, and your enthusiasm is increased by speaking the words. When you do so, the life you want must manifest. Your thought of beauty and goodness for yourself is what determines what you become when you act on it.

Your thinking builds or destroys you. It is a weapon, which by faith accomplishes all things. It is evil, and it is good depending on how you use it. Your thought is so powerful you can't even begin to comprehend or imagine how dynamic it is.

Your thought like air gives you the power and motivate you to do what is good. Your thoughts will lift you to a higher level and make you fly as far as you can go when you think right.

Like the principle of aerodynamics as stated by an instructor in a class that I took. Air is basically what makes an airplane lift off the ground into the sky and fly to a designated destination and back.

In reference to your thinking, your thoughts are actions and the force that motivates you to do the things that are good for you. Your thoughts will work for you as the principle of aerodynamics works for the airplane.

The law of aerodynamics, as I recall in a flight training class, states that the air near the earth's surface is compressed and has more "weight" than air higher in the atmosphere. Air is made up of gasses which have substances. An airplane consists of various materials, and since all substance has weight, an airplane has weight.

The weight of an aircraft keeps it on the ground. In order to fly, the airplane must overcome the weight. Before a plane can fly, it must produce a force greater than its weight. This effect is called 'lift.' Before a plane flies, the lift must be greater than the weight. To generate lift, the aircraft must utilize the air in the atmosphere. The air flowing around the wing of an airplane produces lift. When the wing is moving through the air, the air divides and flows around it. The bottom of the wing pushes down on the air. Air resists crowding and pushes back the airplane. This action produces lift.

An airplane lifts only if the wing moves through the air. The power to move the airplane is produced by the engines, and this is called thrust. To move the airplane, the engine must produce thrust. To move the aircraft fast enough to generate lift, the engines must produce adequate thrust.

Newton's Third Law of Motion tells us that: "Every action produces a reaction equal in force and opposite in direction." "Every Action has an Equal and Opposite Reaction."

The air exhausted from a jet engine is an action and produces a result opposite in direction. The escaping air or movement is toward the rear and thrust or reaction is in a forward direction. The result is also called thrust. To move the airplane forward, the plane must have thrust. To overcome the weight of the aircraft, the plane must lift. The lift is produced by air flowing over and under the wing, and air is a substance and has weight.

How does the repeated illustration correlate with what I am saying in regards to your thought? It is simple. Let's say your body or reality of life, for example, is like an airplane. Your mind is the engine that processes your thoughts and gives you the energy to be creative. Thought has weight and this weight could also parallel the issues of life in your experience that have been weighing your body down. For example, negative thoughts or unproductive thoughts have weight.

The way to move forward and away from what may be weighing you down is to be aware of the thrust; your power.

The power within you to be creative and how your mind works in correlation with that creative thought. The power within you will always work for you when you do what is right. So, you have to think bigger and better thoughts that will lift you out of despondency. When you think good thoughts, you are encouraged to act; when you act, you move forward.

Your thinking can produce joy as well as sadness. You can only move forward when you are free from the thoughts that are weighing you down, the negative pattern of thinking.

The power within you is always life-ward and moves forward. When you habitually feed your mind positive thoughts, it would produce for you positive energy that will cause you to do what is right. Lift in this sense is the reactive energy moving you forward and upward by doing and acting out your creative energy. Putting in energy of good thinking activates your creativity, and when you continue to think right of yourself, you will move upward and forward.

You can only fly high and remain there when you have overcome what is weighing you down, by not focusing on negative thoughts about yourself or others. Negative thought habits will keep you grounded and you cannot produce anything life worthy when you are laden with thought patterns that are not constructive for you. When you decide to move forward by changing your thought habits; replace the old with new and healthy thought patterns, then the weight of the past, dead habits will fall off and the freedom from them will propel you forward.

This is how the law of your mind works, what you put in will come back to you regardless of whether it is positive or negative. Habitual patterns of continued positive thinking might be new to you if you've been laden with thought habits that have been destructive. But when you continue to think right about yourself, the force of what is life-ward and good in those thoughts will eventually lift you, and move you forward to a greater awareness of new experiences and actions. The airplane can only lift up and fly because the thrust is greater than the drag.

You can only move forward when you become aware of what can propel you forward. When you consciously believe that the truth in joy is stronger than the reality of your sad feelings, you will overcome that which is not true, that which has kept you bound when you THINK right and believe in the goodness of your thinking. When the air is not circulating properly, the airplane will not fly properly. When your real thought is burdened by the drag, the negatives, you cannot do anything meaningful.

The airplane passing through the air creates friction. This friction holds the airplane back from moving through the air. If the drag is too great, the aircraft cannot fly.

Smooth surfaces on the plane give the air little to stick to and helps prevent drag. Whenever you decide to do what is right for your upward mobility, there will be a force; a thought trying to hold you back from doing what is right for you. The secret also is that you must press on or else the force of that which is not true will hold you back from fulfilling the truth of what it is you want to do. In reference to the plane, the drag tries to hold and pull the airplane backward, but with the power of the engine thrusting, the plane moves forward.

The captain of the airplane continues to apply the force needed to push the aircraft forward. This is also what you will do when you've decided to do what is right for your success. You must follow through and continue to do that until you've completed what is required of that thought decision.

The air in any living body will choke the individual if it's not circulating properly. When your thoughts are not in harmony, you feel restless, and sometimes you feel pain because you are holding onto thoughts that have hurtful emotions. Thoughts such as guilt, resentment, hate, anger, self-doubt and jealousy are emotions that will weigh you down. When you are bogged down with emotionalized thoughts such as hate and anger, you cannot be happy or free, and when you are not free psychologically, you become depressed and sometimes neurotic. There is hope when an individual recognizes this fact and changes his negative thought habits to constructive positive habits; the new thoughts, like the air, will move the person forward and upward.

The "Law of Motion" states that every action produces an equal and opposite reaction. Your thinking habit is an action, whether positive or negative, will produce for you the experiences of what you either want or don't want. When you change your thought actions, let's say the negative thought actions that you know are not productive; you will receive a reaction, forward movement. Escaping air, according to the principle of aerodynamics is an action that produces a reaction that produces thrust for the plane to move forward and upward. Forgetting what is behind, what is not good for you and moving forward will free you from the effects of their negativity. Each time you want to do what is right and constructive to propel you forward, there will always be a force that will try to keep you from doing what is right, but you must press on with the good thoughts.

There will always be a drag in every man's life when you are trying to do what is good. Negative forces such as doubts, fear or anger, may enter into your mind and may keep you grounded and away from your goal. The mistake many people make is that they allow the negatives to stay too long, that they begin to entertain and believe its doubt and fear, and, therefore, refuse to do what they initially wanted to do. Sometimes unconsciously, you now begin to think that what is good is not for you.

When you think about what is always contrary to good, it keeps you rooted in negativity. The negative thoughts or the drag that pulls you back is what tries to negate what is good in you.

You are not bad because you think negatively or because the pull exists. The fact is you don't know it, and so you think that you are bad or lack the power and resources to do what is right.

The drag will always be there; the thoughts that judge and condemn what is good and progressive in you will always be there. Doubt will rise up if you are not focusing on what is positive to achieve. The truth is, you must continue to thrust forward if you want to lift up and fly. Don't listen to the negatives or lag behind in the drag. Move forward like an airplane that must push forward in order that it can create thrust for lifting and flying in the sky to its destination.

The airplane is in the sky because the air on the surface of the earth is thin, and this air keeps the plane moving and lifting because the aircraft is thrusting. Your continuous effort to do what is right will eventually become drag resistant because you are continuously on a different thought level that is always constructive. The drag will always be there, but it will not be strong enough to pull you down and keep you grounded in the negative.

Air has weight; it circulates in you and gives life, or you die from lack of it. Your thought has weight, and if what you are thinking are positive and constructive, it will elevate you to a new level. Your thought like a mass of compressed air will also pull you down. The way you react to expectations in life can be burdensome and can sometimes leave you depleted and unproductive. To sum up everything regarding the thought of man as the power source that moves his world; let us see what Apostle Paul said in Romans.

In the book of Romans, Chapter 12:2; Apostle Paul advised the believers of Christ to "offer their bodies as a living sacrifices; holy and pleasing to God. " This is a spiritual act of worship to God and is the only acceptable gift a man can give to God.

"Do not conform to the pattern of this world any longer," he said to them, "rather be transformed by the renewing of your mind. Then will you be able to test and approve what God's will is, his good and perfect will for you that is forever pleasing." Apostle Paul's advice to the Gentiles is still relevant today.

The 'bodies that are offered as sacrifice' Apostle Paul is talking about is not the physical body, but the mind-body which can also be interpreted as the church; the faith which you are, the consciousness or thought of man. This should be kept holy and pure; for this is the only offering a man can give to the creator of his soul.

THE LAW OF YOUR BEING IS YOUR THOUGHT

◇ ◇ ◇ ◇ ◇

Your thought is the law of your being. The idea of yourself, your response to the world should be of love. When you think harmoniously, then, as 'Apostle Paul said, "you can test what is always good within you and prove it yourself," because then what you say, or think in your (garden) mind, according to what is true within you, will be true and right as it has been from the beginning.

Every thought that forms in your mind is a law, and the effect of that law is a circumstance you feel or find yourself in. Let us take a hypothetical example: A young man commits a serious crime that sends him to jail. Let's face it, in every society there are laws that protect its citizens, and when you break the law of a society, there are consequences. Sometimes the punishment is life imprisonment if not death in some countries. Subsequently, every thought is bound by natural law. Sometimes individual decisions keep one in a mental prison.

And sometimes the only way to get out of such a bind or mindset and out of the law restricting you is an awareness that your thinking got you into the mindset in the first place. You accepted a thought process that put you in a very difficult life situation.

The moment that you realized you did something wrong and have acknowledged your responsibility for your wrong actions; that thought or moment gives you an outlet from feeling bad and allows you to get unchained out of the laws of your mind. The acknowledgment of the act provides you with the option to release yourself from feeling sad and guilty.

Your thought of feeling happy frees you from being sad, and that subsequently frees your mind. That is, mentally you have been liberated from the law that binds you, but there are still consequences associated with the societal rules that you have broken. You have to serve the punishment; then again, you can be pardoned and forgiven.

This is where some would say, "Ah, he is so lucky. Do you know that the judge let him out of jail, just like that?"

You can be released from prison for good behavior. Or your sentence is reduced because you have a good attorney, and you are pardoned ultimately by the natural laws of forgiveness which some State laws acknowledge and enact.

The truth is that you began that process in your mind and you sent out the signals unconsciously, and eventually it was caught by someone coming to your defense. The judge pardoned you based on laws that say; you can be forgiven because you served some time.

You were a real person that made ill-thought decisions. Liberating ourselves from the laws of our actions comes when we also shift the way we think about the situations in which we find ourselves. Let's look at another hypothetical example: You made a choice to move into a neighborhood, but after moving in, you realized you didn't like the apartment and the neighborhood. You couldn't move out right away because you signed a new lease, and you don't have the money to move into a new place. The freedom you experience was when you realized you could change the situation.

In this case, there are different options for getting out of the situation. You can break the lease and lose your security deposit, or speak to your landlord to see if he can get you out of that lease with no penalty. Your understanding of the fact that you can change the situation eliminates the degree of worry on your part and at the same time allowing you the time to change your thinking which is what initially created the circumstances that you found yourself in.

You might now say, you don't have the money to move into a new environment. Here is the key: The reason you find yourself in the present situation is that you created the thoughts that brought you into the house that you are now living in. It also follows that you can use the same pattern (which is your thinking) to create a new environment that you wish to live in, and the money needed to move you into a new environment will come.

All you have to do is create a new picture of what you want. If you don't have a picture of what you want, look around, look in the Newspaper, News Magazine, or on-line and search for what appeals to you, and see it in your mind. When you do this, you can begin to recreate a feeling for yourself, and in time, you will change your situation. Regarding living in an apartment that you don't like, the law of that thought is the feeling associated with the environment that you find yourself in.

How do you free yourself from the consequences of that law? You become free from the law that binds you presently when you realize that you can also change your situation by changing your thinking. Every thought is action, and every action is bound by law when acted out. In the case where the thought or action broke an inserted law, (such as thou shall not commit murder) you will serve the consequences for breaking that law. Even when society does not have a functioning law, there is still a natural law and its reciprocal effect that follows your chain of thoughts. In this case, there is something called associated laws, laws that eventually catch up with you, and ultimately will either destroy you or, in this instance, put you in a bind. Unless you recognize what binds you, you will continue to experience difficulty. Remember, thoughts are actions; thoughts are things and every action or word is a law to itself.

LIFE IS ABOUT DECISIONS

❖ ❖ ❖ ❖ ❖

Some of the things that have happened to you today or in the past are based on the decisions you've made or that others have made for you that you believed and acted upon. Some of your life experiences, whether good or bad, came about through your decisions or actions and some from your environment. When I say some, I am speaking of the age of discernment. You might not believe this, but you are in control of your success or lack of it. If you are in control of what happens to you by the way you think; then you should endeavor to make good decisions about the actions you take based on your thoughts; because it is your pattern of thinking and action that determines what becomes of you. If you are not satisfied with the way your life is going right now, you have the power and choice to make it different.

The gift of life is already yours and it is up to you to decide the kind of life you choose to live. When I sat down to reexamine my life and analyze each phase that I felt was hurtful or problematic and challenging, I realize they were so because of the way I thought about them or related to them. I came to the understanding that it is the emotions attached to each of this perceived hurting event that made me sad or troubled. I made a conscious decision to change the way I thought and reacted to incidents in my life. If I don't like the way I feel about a situation that my decision created, I stop the feelings attached to that situation.

The ultimate changer is not to repeat the decision if I didn't like the way I felt afterward about it. The healer is that I just had to come up with a different way of dealing with the situation and learn what that situation teaches me. So, if your past actions have led you to where you think you are stuck, in some sort of bondage, there is hope as long as you use your mind and change the way you think.

You can start by careful visualization, change the things that have held you bound through your thought patterns, by changing your perspective of the things that are not in harmony with you, and visualizing how you want it to be. The decisions you make in the course of your daily encounters in life determine the path in which you travel. No other person can make your journey through life successful but you. Through the decisions you make every day for yourself, you will determine for yourself what you want to be.

To accomplish any dream in life, you have to see that which you want to be or where you wish to see yourself, then set out to do things that are necessary for the fulfillment of that dream. What are your dreams? Do you want to be a carpenter, electrician, a medical doctor, a lawyer, a musician, or a pianist, an astronaut or a pilot? Whatever it is that you want to do, find out what is necessary for accomplishing that dream and set forth to pursue it. Don't let anyone distract or stop you from achieving that which your heart yearns to have.

Set a goal and deadline and then follow through with it. Without that, you will keep finding yourself in the same cycle of discontent about your lifestyle over and over again.

Decisions are the ultimate determinant of any outcome in life. When we think, we are settings things in motion, and the effect of that mental decision is the circumstance we find ourselves in. Though many people are not aware of this force, it is very true. The choices we make are accomplished by deciding to follow-thru with a decision or not.

When we decide to choose one thing over the other, say a path to the highway, the consequences are what we experience on that road. Whatever thing we encounter in the way we've chosen to the highway is what we feel, see, and live through, until we decide to make another change. The wise choice will be to make a decision about your thought pattern and choose another highway if the pathway you choose is not where you wish to be.

As a child, you were helpless in making decisions. Thus, your parents or guardians made decisions they thought best for you- decisions that you obeyed and acted upon. As you grow into adulthood, the responsibility is shifted to you to decide and choose. The individual who must now make constructive decisions about what to do in life is you.

It is a fact that some adults as children might have experienced abuse; such as physical, verbal or emotional abuse from their parent or guardians. Therefore, the effects of the environment they grew up in and the abuse they received may prompt them to act out their experiences in negative ways.

It is really unfortunate that it happened, but there is hope for those who want to get out of that cycle of anger and sadness from their past. The good news is that, although the past experiences might not be forgotten, the way these experiences are viewed and sometimes expressed can be changed for the better through a change in the thought process. It might take twice as much effort with help from professional counselors for those who were badly hurt. But it is possible that any person can also change their thought patterns to a life of pleasure and happiness if the person really wants to make a change.

With proper counseling, an individual can gradually break free from the effects of his negative childhood experience and live the rest of his life in glorious bliss and joy. But the decision must be made to live differently from the past. Decisions, whether conscious or not, are the sole reasons we experience failure or success in life. Decisions are like markers that we walk on.

And they don't have to be permanent if they have caused us pain instead of joy because everyone has been given the secret weapon to change. This is the ability to choose again and to think differently. You can again decide for yourself how to live your life when you take control of your thoughts as long as you are alive. It is not an easy task, but it can be done, just as effortlessly as the negative thought that has taken shape in your mind.

My high school principal once told me and my fellow classmates that we are the architects of our destiny. I still remember the effects of those words like it was yesterday. Because each time I think of those words, they still motivate me to want to do, and be a better human being. How true that concept was then when my high school principal said it in the assembly hall more than twenty-five years ago. I have come to realize that in my moments of frustration, anger, stress or fear, these were the moments that I made the decisions that may have altered my life experiences.

Many of the painful and happy memories of my high school and college years, I realized stemmed from the decisions that I made at each moment or prior to the events taking place.

Your character or your experiences are made by the decisions of the past and thus determines your future. Like fossils and limestone in the depths of the earth whose formations occurred through layers of dead animals and leaves, so too are the thoughts that formed you. The decision and choice of the past made consciously or unconsciously are what you are.

The cultural self that some people claim to be, the 'who that they are' came about by generational decisions of their parents, grandparents and societal laws. Your thoughts whether conscious or unconscious are the pattern that has been either in your favor or have worked against you.

The good news is that it can be changed when you become aware of its hindrance in your life and decide to change the way you view life. Many people don't seem to realize the effect of their thoughts on their life and some who do, don't want to take action. By doing nothing, they succumb to the lifestyle they think can't be changed. What they don't know is that their thought patterns can change everything they saw as impossible.

Interestingly, people are so used to the patterns of behavior inherited from the past that the decision to do nothing has also added to the distorted pattern of the past. This is the demotivating factor in what they are experiencing, the frustrations of how they see their life.

The real self that is the image of God is forever true; the pure self that we ought and need to express is hidden inside. How can you express this self? You can express this real self by thinking positively about yourself and the world around you, and by taking action and implementing change where change is needed.

Your parents' decisions to have you either consciously or unconsciously led to you being born. You become the result of their actions. Now whether you were supposed to be here or not, that is no longer an issue. You were born and you have a purpose of being. The issue is you are here; you have a life and you have the right of a living being to express what is true in you through your thought pattern.

This thinking is not forceful. It is effortlessly carried out by what is already true in you. It becomes an effort if the thought is faulty. This is when you now make an effort to change the way you see things. The new you can also begin with your decision to become a different person, the person you envisioned being from the moment you decided to change your thinking about yourself.

If you are not happy with the person you see daily, change that view and see who you want to become: then take the steps necessary to realize that vision. If you recall, I asked you to picture the person you wish to see or things that might change the way you feel about yourself. When you closed your eyes and visualized that one person or thing you want to see or have, you felt the presence of your choice. The presence was real in your mind because of your belief or thought pattern.

So if your choice of the person became real in your conceptual world, it could also become real in your visual world when that picture is grasped continuously. Visible things of the world come into being from the notion of it.

You can become a different person the moment you consciously decide you've had enough pain from your present condition. When you believe in the essence of your new conceptual image, it will manifest as your new present experience. If this picture is an idea of service to you and others, ways and options will present themselves on how to accomplish that which you have thought of. Follow this option, all it takes is the first step to pursue what it is you what to be. The decision will jar you a little bit, which is the truth that you are doing the right thing.

Old habits are sometimes hard to break. They fight to remain in you, and unless you are determined to get rid of that old habit, it will stay in you and act out through you. When you visualize a right image of yourself, believe it, act on the insight that comes from it, and it will become real for you. Begin now to choose what kind of thoughts you will dwell on. You can start to affirm your wholeness as a creature of the Almighty God. You can begin by concentrating on pure thoughts because they are life forces that build your continuous experience, the grooves they establish on the base of your subconscious mind become a pattern that moves and guides you to do what is always good.

The base of your thinking mind could be likened to a plastic cushion that carries you each day; like an automatic reflex, even when you are not thinking, it bounces up to tell you what you need to do and know. As such, dwelling on thoughts of anger or fear also creates a groove in the seat of your mind. These thoughts come back to you as experiences of distress, discomfort, sadness, and negative actions that prompt you to exhibit more negative actions and reactions. A prolonged state of grief, when not counteracted by creative and positive thoughts, becomes an emotional depression.

The choice is yours to make a decision based on your thoughts. Your thoughts are behavior and the effects through your reaction or experiences. Your subconscious mind, the seat on which your thinking is based, is given to you freely by the creator of your being.

I know it's often difficult to discipline yourself from being offended or letting other people's criticism hurt and create offense in your heart. The truth of the matter is, once you begin to focus on the offense, you are actually creating a future experience of sorrow and anxiety for yourself. If this has been a problem for you in the past, if you are always chewing on words thrown at you by people to offend you, I urge you to refuse those thoughts of anger. Rather, replace them with loving thoughts of forgiveness for the individual who hurt you and also for yourself.

This exercise might appear to be childish, but this is the power to control your world. When positive constructive thoughts are consistently repeated, they become effortless as time moves on. Positive thoughts will begin to bounce up spontaneously in your mind, and no longer will you feel the residual effect of your negative thoughts.

It is not easy to break the pattern of thinking which one did not even realize was the tapestry of their existence in life, but it can be done with effort and sometimes effortlessly. You can re-establish the freedom in your life when you take control of your thoughts. The easiest way to check your thoughts is to verify the feelings associated with the thoughts that come into your mind.

Analyze every thought to see if it is of any benefit to you and others. When you get angry at an offense committed against you, take a moment to look consciously at it before you react, by evaluating the reason you are getting angry.

Ask yourself: Is the issue worth getting angry over and what will it accomplish for me? Will it fulfill my desire of peace? If the answer is no, then there is absolutely no reason why you should be angry. No one else is feeling the anxiety or the residual effect of bitter thoughts in your body but you. So, is it worth it to boil over in anger? I don't think so! If you take a look at the problem at hand, you will find out that the underlying factor in your anger is really self-pride; your ego and nothing else.

Our feeling of anger is sometimes the consequence of wanting to be heard or acknowledged and when we don't get that response from the other party, who also wishes to be heard and recognized; we respond negatively, by reacting angrily.

You felt slighted and disrespected because your need to be heard or understood and accepted were ignored. The fact is, if you had accomplished your goal to be heard or appreciated like you wanted to, you'd feel satisfied and contented. So what is really at risk here is your ego? Nobody wants to be ignored or disrespected. Everyone wants to be validated by people they relate to.

Every thinking man is actually seeking one thing, among many, and that is, to be recognized and to show how good he or she is. When that factor is ignored, the individual takes it personally and tries to find ways to be acknowledged or ways to reprimand or snub the other person who has ignored him.

The self that wants to be publicly acknowledged is the person that sometimes must submit, and in doing so the real you will emerge. The true you cannot get offended because no one can really hurt the true you, it does not argue but withdraws when it is not listened to. Goodness does not need to prove its worth. It is already good, and already present. Your real self is irresistible.

Every reasoning person should be in control of his thought and his reactions to other peoples' ideas because that is the only way he is able to guard against negative forces that want to enter into his mind. Your response to any attitude directed towards you is the control you have over what thoughts come to you every minute of your waking hour. You are the architect of your destiny; therefore, have your thoughts channeled to a place you want to live in. Your thought should be the sap of peace and love for yourself and others.

When you think good thoughts towards people everywhere, even those you don't consider friends, the effortless presence of your good ideas will create new experiences for you. Good thought habits create a bridge of harmony for your soul, thus creating a free path to communication with God.

Stop lying, cheating and bearing false witness. Stop being deceptive, resentful and unforgiving. When you don't, these forces become the elements that prevent the power of positive creativity. This is because a heart filled with lovely thoughts is a heart that is undoubtedly connected to God. Thoughts that are pure and without negative feelings of hate and resentment are the life force of strength that motivates you to do things.

We are placed upon this earth to do the will of our Creator, which is to live joyously, free and productive. An orange tree fulfills the will of its creator by bearing fruits which is its purpose.

It is my choice to share this revelation with you because keeping it to myself would not fulfill its purpose, which is that knowledge is gained when expressed and shared. The purpose of education is intended to enlighten the mind that takes it in so that it can build relations. When you have the right knowledge, your mind regenerates and brings to light those words of purity, the truth in the universe that are hidden and trampled upon by choices of false generational thinking.

Negative and angry thought patterns impede your access to Godly thoughts. When you are angry or think distortedly, your mind becomes clogged up. The freedom to think correctly becomes challenging, thus hindering the natural flow of kindness, love, peace, creativity and good that is in you.

Your purpose in life is to bring forth that which is good in yourself and in others so that together you can create a beautiful world for yourself and others to live in. The tangible things that make life easy to live in is mans' creation.

This visible world and consumable things in it was once thought. The things you see around you were once force or energy floating in space until it was conceived of and brought forth to fruition through the power of God residing in man through his thoughts. How could that be, only by dwelling on what is always right and love? Whatever the mind conceives and the heart believes, it comes into being through your actions.

When you believe in what is good, the truth of what you believe becomes a power in you, thereby making you act the way your mind perceived it. As you have noticed, this process is carried by the choice and decision to accept that which was given freely. Pure and honest decisions build up a deposit of life forces, which give you confidence or low self-esteem and then eventually becomes the character self.

As one chooses the house he lives in, the clothes he wears and food he eats, that is how the choice of his thoughts determines what he experiences each day. Unfortunately, some people are not aware of this and are not living in the expectation of what is good in them, because of lack of knowledge of who they are as a dominant thought being.

The Christ that dwells in your heart is the truth and life that you must believe in. The truth of who you are, the original presence that was and is without inhibition the life force, (the Word, and the image of God) that bore every man. Every thought like doubts and fears are variations of things, like reflection of what is not. Fear, for example, is what is not, fear is a shadow.

An illustration of fear is somewhat similar to the reflection that comes out when one sees a shadow against the wall, the real you is behind the shadow. That shadow is not a real person but a shadow against the wall. Now do you believe in the darkness or the truth in the person standing in front of the wall?

Though the truth is an unseen presence, it is just as real as you are true. It becomes manifest in your daily experiences when you are aware of it and its goodness for you. The presence that regulates the life in you can heal you and cause every wrong done to you to be removed only when you trust it to do what you have desired.

When you believe in the truth in you regardless of what the external says, you can and will accomplish whatever you set your mind to achieve, because you are a replication of God, the image of what is always true.

Believe in the essence of what was in the beginning, the Christ in your heart, and it will give you peace and strength, compelling you to reach a higher level of conscious awareness.

Fear has no principle, but faith and truth do. Fear will cease being with you when you stop focusing your thought or energy on negative emotions. The truth of what is right for you; the life force that gives you power and nourishes your bone as it regenerates the blood cells in your body and heals your wound is your gift and the power that you must believe in. The choice is yours and the decision, yours.

WHO IS THE ENEMY

❖❖❖❖❖❖

Who are your enemies? You probably have a list of names of enemies; actual people that you think did you wrong. Who are the real demons? Where do you think you can find the real enemy? I tell you not very far. The real enemy is next to you, seating as close as you can ever imagine. Take a look once more around you. Do you think you have an enemy troubling you? Think again. Who are your enemies?

I guess you are now thinking real names, feelings that associate with real hurt. This question has made you think of all the verbs or nouns related to the word pain. When you feel pain and anger because of people's behavior towards you, they were not caused by the people whom you interacted with.

The real enemies are not people; the real enemies are your thoughts, your reactions, the way you responded to behaviors, the negative responses that you entertained in your mind. Your distorted thoughts are the real enemy.

They are just as physical as you want them to be. You are responsible for controlling your negative thinking because you created them; you fashioned the Frankenstein that disturbs you, the one you call enemy. You allowed it inside of you. Someone might have sent you a missile-like force of negative energy, if you did not accept it or ruminate on it, it would not have offended or cause you to react in such a way that it hurts you. If you did not accept it, then it could never harm you. Your enemies are your negative thoughts; the hurtful way you think about something.

The attitude of the mind depends on what we believe. Therefore, the secret of all power, all achievement and possession depends upon our method of thinking. You must "be" before you can "do, and you can only do to the extent which you "are," and what you "are" depends on what you "think and feel."

Your mind is creative. The conditions, environment and all expectation of life are the results of your habitual or predominant mental attitude. All the annoying thoughts your mind has ever conceived or accepted have taken the place of the real feelings and are the demons that trouble you. Your unfulfilled desires too can become frustrations and pain, and pattern of thoughts and behaviors. The thought of not realizing your desires has been in your mind and has become emotionalized negatively in your heart for too long that it caused your pain. Sometimes these pain can be felt all over your body. The Pain comes about when there is a lack of oxygen in the body because of the negative emotion which is stored up in your body. And where there is a lack of oxygen in your arteries, there will be pain due to shock and stiffness because of lack of blood with oxygen, which was caused by a blockage in the thinking. Change your thoughts and entertain what is good, and the enemies will flee from you. Your enemies will submit themselves to you, when you dwell on that which is pure and good.

This time you can control that which you entertain, by entertaining only what is good for you. The Christ in you is the foundation that you need to consider, the truth of your life. The goodness in you is the thought you must dwell on. There is power in that goodness and that power is real. The presence of Christ in you is the pure force that will nourish and give you confidence. The absence of faith bridges fear, and fear sets in motion the irresponsible decisions, making you believe that there was something; wrong when your thought was the culprit.

You are afraid of your feelings when you allow negative thoughts to dominate your mind. The way you think, and the grudges you bear in your mind are the real enemies that stop you in the track of success. I am sure you know that whatever thought your mind conjures and your heart believes, sets the foundation for action. Whatever you become aware of, manifests in the natural, which becomes your experience.

If you have a fearful thought of somebody, the thought of that person becomes a realization of an actual person tormenting you or making you angry. This is because you've entertained thoughts about this person that are not positive. Your view has taken the persona of people you perhaps have problems with in the past. That can change if you focus your mind on what is good. When you think of what is lovely, it will produce a feeling of loving reactions, effects or experiences that become an inspiration to motivate you to act in love.

When you believe on an action verb that is negative, it produces emotion. Harmful thinking acts as a deterrent, it wasn't meant to be entertained any more than the second it was perceived. Therefore, after you've perceived it, disregard it as false. Negative things are not life; it means they are non- existent but have life because we give them meaning. So why do people still believe in the negatives? It has to do with many things such as habits; but mainly because that's all they've been unconsciously motivated and trained to believe as such. The negative becomes a force that compels and moves them to act from the negative perspective.

The negative should only act as a deterrent and to encourage you, its effects should prompt you to do what is right and proper. When you make a mistake, you should not condemn yourself, or dwell on thoughts about yourself that are inferior.

When you condemn or think falsely about yourself, you hinder your ability to think creatively and the longer you believe in this false concept, the real it becomes for you.

When you don't stop thinking falsely about yourself, you will begin to act according to the way you've visualized yourself in your mind. The falseness wasn't the original truth but became the truth because you believed it. Believing is the way you see and think. The original good word is now hidden amidst the distorted patterns, which you didn't realize is the new you that is causing your discomfort. When you believe or think what is false, it takes on a personality or force and that force compels you to act according to its truth.

An illustration of how the negatives work is parallel to the electric charge that has positive and negative sides. The negative charges are not meant to be played with, and likewise your negative thoughts. The thoughts that are in your mind constantly are not to be expressed or retained if they are negative.

The negative thoughts were intended to bolster the positive in order that the functions of the active thoughts are carried out through your positive actions. The electric wire, when charged and exposed, is dangerous. If you touch a live electric wire, it can harm you. This illustration parallels your mental concept of negative and positive thoughts.

The negative thoughts as real forces will prompt you to act accordingly, by you conceiving and believing on adverse effects that will then cause you to do what it wants. Fear will keep you locked up and confused.

Several years ago, a young lady whom I befriended was obsessed with the fear of the disease Acquired Immune Deficiency Syndrome (AIDS) after she had taken the test that proved negative. Even after taking the test and she knew she had no reason to fear, she was still obsessed with the fear of this disease. Why was she so afraid? She was scared because she had harbored the thought of illness. Unfortunately for her, based on the natural law of the thoughts in her mind, her fearful thoughts began to produce symptoms like someone who was seriously ill.

She said she had chills, sweats at night, fever, cold and pain all over her body, especially within her knee joints. She also had fatigue and was constantly tired. Sometimes she could barely stand for more than a minute before sitting down.

She thought she was going to die, and her negative thought pattern continued for several months. She said she found herself acting like she was sick and even took caution not to harm anyone by not visiting friends. She refused to come to my apartment and even went as far as writing a goodbye letter to her parents.

Luckily she did not mail the letter to her parents. And though she was afraid, she was also eager to get well from such debilitating fear. Fear will make you do things that are very wrong.

As my friend wanted to get out of the predicament that she was in, she continually prayed and went to group meetings for people with the same kind of pain that she was experiencing. It was then that she realized that what she had was actually called an anxiety attack. An attack which was provoked by a traumatic experience she had with a police officer arresting her at her place of work.

At the time, she thought she was going to be deported back to her country for not renewing her visa. An Anxiety attack can be provoked by any incident and for my friend, it was prompted by the thought of being deported. When you live in the spirit of truth that is Christ, the power which is Christ can also protect you who believe in it and thereby prevent you from getting in harm's way.

One might ask, but how about the innocent children who are with these diseases and are dying from it? Why isn't that the power that is good preventing them from this illness? Unfortunately, it is not their fault, neither the responsibility of their parents, but circumstances. The power of Christ, which is good is still forever within the innocent child; though he or she might have gotten sick through an action that isn't his.

If a child is consciously aware of the presence of faith in him, or if someone can visualize healing for the child, the child will get well. We are conscious of the actions of many well-meaning doctors and citizens around the globe who have dedicated their life's work to helping those stricken with the disease. Their work with the assistance of modern medicine have improved the lives of many children who were born with it, and many have been immune from the disease due to improvementS in medicine.

These good Samaritans visualized helping the people stricken with this disease and did something about it. And because of their actions, things are happening; many with this illness are living longer because they are getting treatments.

The actions of these well meaningful Samaritans somewhat mirrors the faith that stands in the gap for others that may not have faith strong enough to heal themselves. The young lady experienced anxiety attackS triggered by fear, which was triggered by thoughts she allowed her mind to entertain. Her healing came only when she realized that her pain was caused by her thoughts. The moment she realized this, the process of her healing from the panic attack began. Without understanding the way her mind worked, she couldn't have gotten rid of the fear in her mind.

The fear of such disease came about because she had always dwelt on negative thoughts about this illness and nothing else. She changed the way she felt about herself in relation to the disease when she became aware of what the enemy was. She released the thoughts that had gripped her mind with fear and the enemy fled.

She had to do something about her thought pattern because she knew she did not want to live in fear any longer. She was prompted to take the test again. In fact, she took it three times, thereby confronting the fears head on; since taking the test was what provoked the initial fear in her. She had to die to the fear of believing falsely by believing the good within her that makes all things new. Though she panicked every time she hears a discussion about this disease on television, she reaffirmed what was good within her by saying the words below out loud.

"The goodness of the Lord is within me. I am filled with peace, and I have a healthy mind and body. I am good always." She had to deal with her fear by confessing what is true, which was her health. And she also focused on what was good within her. She thought good and lovely thoughts, things she wanted to do that had value. She overcame the fear she had of the disease by replacing the negative thoughts with beliefs of the truth of health.

She rid herself of the fear of this disease because she refused to believe anything else for herself, but the rightness which she was. She believed in that which was right of her, which was the goodness that is resident in her. That is why we have to be careful of what we hear and ruminate on because what we think and meditate on often sink into our heart as ideas and experiences.

Though the good in us is always true, we also have to be wise to listen and obey the voice within us to do what is good and right and guard ourselves with the right thoughts. You are unwise when you don't act according to what is good and right within you. Having a careless sexual encounter outside a proper relationship because everyone has it or because you are pressured into doing so is not constructive for you. And neither is having sex because you are under the influence of some external force such as drugs or alcohol.

Although the goodness in you does not want you to condemn yourself when you make a mistake; it also wants you to be wise and refrain from doing what you know does not agree with the truth within you. The truth is that when the good in you is listened to and obeyed, it will guard you in every action you take. It will prompt you to do only what is good for you and what is good for others.

In terms of being afraid of doing what your heart truly desires, what is good in you will liberate you and motivate you to do whatever you may fear, therefore causing the fear to disappear. I didn't learn how to drive until I was thirty years old because of fear. I was so afraid of driving that I did not think I could ever drive a car. Sometimes I would refuse to ride in the front seat of any car for fear of an accident. I was so afraid that each time I rode in the front seat of a car I would begin to critique the driver on how he was driving. Sometimes, when I sat in the front passenger seat of a car, I would catch myself pressing my foot hard on the floor of the car because I was afraid that the driver would have an accident. I don't think my action would have stopped an accident from happening, but fearfull thoughts made me do it.

I couldn't go on like that if I ever wanted to learn how to drive a car. And so I had to do something about my fear. I once heard someone say, do what you are afraid of the most and the death of that thing is certain.

I began to see myself driving all the time in my mind. One day I managed to plead with a friend to let me drive her car in a parking lot. The first time I sat in a car determined to learn how to drive was the day I conquered my fear of driving. A few months later I managed to get a small loan from my employer to buy a car. When I bought my car, I still did not know how to drive, but the underlying truth was I wanted to learn how to drive a car.

I didn't want to believe the fear that I couldn't drive. And even though I had a car, I still could not drive it. I had parked the car on the side street close to where I lived for weeks. And each time I walked past it in the morning on my way to work, I saw myself driving it. Though I took the train every time I went to work, I believed one day that I was going to drive my car.

I honestly didn't know how that would happen since I couldn't even afford paying for driving lessons. But I was unwavering in my thought to learn how to drive by the strength of God in me. On my way home one morning from work, I made up my mind that I was going to drive my car that day. Though I was physically tired and needed some sleep after long hours of working the previous day, I was as determined as ever to drive.

I had an inspiration that morning. I felt a sense of elevation in me to do what I had envisioned, and that was to drive. I had the strength in me that I didn't want to waste. The strength I had came from believing in the truth; the possibility that I could drive. I got into my parked car that morning and began to drive. Mind you the first time I ever entered a car and turned a car wheel was in the parking lot with a friend, several weeks prior.

I believe that when one is ready to break a negative behavior, which is really a pattern of thought one has cultivated for a long period, the person will succeed because the power to do so comes from doing. That morning I stepped into my car and drove my car for nearly one hour. I drove around the neighborhood where I lived. I even drove by a police car and was not afraid. The police officer did not stop me or look at me like I was doing something wrong. That day marked the beginning of my becoming a driver. After several trials, I went to the Department of Motor Vehicle for my driver's license, and I have been driving ever since.

There is strength in you to break any habit, whether of fear or depressive thoughts if you really want to. Fear can only keep you from doing the things you want to do when you dwell on that fear. When you live in fear it becomes false fear, genuine fear is meant to prevent you from harm's way, to protect you from falling or hurting yourself. Fear is not intended to be entertained any longer than the moment it flashed through your mind. When you cease from believing falsely, your confidence grows and your strength to do what is right is built up within you. False fear or self-doubt will keep you from doing the things you most desire because fear is the opposite of faith.

When you conceive and believe on any image whether wrong or real, it becomes for you what you have projected; your belief of what is true. One of the reasons why there are so many people without the things they actually need in life is because they don't know how their subconscious mind works in relation to what they think habitually. They don't know that their thought pattern is what is holding them back from achieving what they actually want.

Negative thoughts weren't meant to be thought on. They come that you might be able to distinguish between what is right for you and what is not. People will always perceive ideas that negate what they see, but it is your responsibility and choice to decide the thought you want to meditate on. Good thoughts will reveal more good ideas to you, and negative thoughts will lead to more negative actions.

When you think on what is positive, it becomes what you feel, see and become until you think of being different. This thought pattern builds and propels you, especially when you act to fulfill the truth of what you thought about.

If the word that is true is not acted upon, it remains docile. To activate it, a person has to act on it. Acting according to the good word, the image of the good in you, builds confidence, which in effect strengthens the individual to do more acts of goodwill.

Successful people are those who believed in the principle of, "I CAN." They felt that they could achieve all their heart had conceived and it became real to them. The truth is that you can do all things through the strength of God in you. But the moment you begin to doubt the essence of the truth of the goodness in you, the false becomes what is true for you because you believed it. The enemies, which you fear, or I feared in the past, were our thoughts and nothing more, and thoughts can be replaced with new vital ideas.

All the negative thoughts you've ever conceived are the troubles in your life. Have you ever wondered why things aren't going the way they should? These inconveniences are the choices you've made until adulthood. These concepts or feelings that are not pleasant change your perception of who you feel you are, and what is not real becomes real because your heart has accepted it. Change your thought and your enemies will flee from you.

One of the teachings of Jesus Christ is for people to love their enemies as equally as their friend because love or hate live within the individual. When you love your friends and hate your enemy, you are diluting the force of love that you've conceived. When you love your friends, you love yourself. When you hate your enemy, you actually hate yourself, because the thought of hate are in your mind, and the truth of the emotions are entertained in your mind and felt in your heart. The power to hate only does what is harmful to you; it taints the mirror of your soul because such energy was never meant for those created in the right image of God. But because so many of us think of what is wrong, these forces have also attracted what is wrong from the outside, thereby causing us to feel hate instead of love, peace, and joy.

The forces of hate only build a blockade to the path of purity from the life-giving power in you, thus creating or forming the continuous character of hate in you. As you know, hate doesn't glow. In the beginning you may feel empowered by the surge, but after a while it becomes a dead force, a deterrent holding you back from growing in the direction of love and peace, that was originally planted in you.

Let the good light live supreme in your heart by having thoughts of love and the forces of good in you will release the presence of joy and peace that will motivate you from hating any person. You may get angry, but it will not penetrate to the depths of your being because the thought, which you choose to dwell on, is love and all that is associated with goodness. Remember this, each time you breathe in clean air, you are being born again.

The new air that you inhale represents the new you and the CO_2 represents the old you. As you have perhaps learned, we exhale carbon dioxide and breathe in oxygen. CO_2 or carbon dioxide is not meant to remain in our system; it was expected to be discharged. Therefore, visualize your thoughts as the fresh air that you breathe. And since the fresh air is like your thought, it is invariably your life.

You don't sit and inhale the dust around you when you are cleaning the house you live in; you try to prevent the dust particles from entering your nostrils. Therefore, you should also do the same with your mental concepts. Try your best not to focus on the negative thought the moment it flashes in your mind.

Every day when you go to sleep and wake up, you are being renewed. Let every day be a new day in your mind as it is new every morning, and as you inhale breath of air, you are renewed and changed. The enemy that you think is alive is actually an inactive thought, a force made live by your choice to feel that it is there. In actuality, it was already forgotten and expelled as the CO_2, which you breathed out.

Your decision to get out of the dusty place changes your awareness of what you can be.

You can't change the past, but you can change what will be by trusting in what is true about the possibility. You can believe the whole, the life that created heaven and earth and in the God, which is within you.

THE PROMISES OF GOD

What is a promise? A promise is a guarantee of what is to come; the continuation of what has been said before. A promise is an expectation of what is good or what was declared; that is, your concept of what is good in you. A promise is something that is certain to come to pass. Invariably faith is what I am talking. Faith is a promise. The promise of God to His children is that they may have life abundantly. Life was announced to the children of Abraham. Life is what is good because life is an image of God and we were made in the image of God.

The image of God is His thought, which is His word; the faith that was used to form all living things that came to pass through his children. God promised every believer of His word on earth His power by the covenant He had at the beginning of creation that through His son, the Word, those who see right have all that is rightly theirs. The truth in the word of God is His Son, and he who believes in His Son also believes in the Father.

The truth of God is His promise, which says, all that God has is ours, His strength is ours, His glory and authority is ours when we abide in his truth. (1 John 2: 24-25) God promised the children of Abraham eternal life if they would abide in his truth and live right. Believe in the truth that is from the beginning, in His son, and thou shall have life abundantly. The promise of God that he would fulfill all that he has begun in you is profound if you will do rightly. Every thought or good idea that will bless you and others is the promise of God to you when you do what is right to accomplish it.

The answer has already been given to you when you obey the commandment from your heart. Every idea that you have ever conceived has a potential for fruition when you believe in its reality. When you believe in the actualization of what you have conceived in your heart, its fulfillment is destined to be when you don't negate it with doubt.

When you negate an idea conceived out of the purity of your heart; the realization is not fulfilled because you've destroyed it in faith. When you negate an image of kindness in your mind, you have killed the essence of its truth. As such, the life that could have come about from that idea becomes a hindrance psychologically, because you suppressed it with doubt and fear.

To gain your freedom, act on the next good idea that you conceived, and the life in that new idea will propel you to resurrect all the other ideas and your freedom to be is certain. When you believe in the possibility of any good idea in your heart, its life force will compel you to do what is necessary that it may come to fruition.

The fulfillment is the truth of the idea. All things are possible when you believe the reality, and the reality of the good you think, is the promise that surely is. When you are conscious of your dreams and you are focused on achieving them, whatever happens on the outside that is not relating to your dreams should not matter to you.

In Genesis 37:5-8; Joseph had a dream and revealed his dreams to his brothers and because of this; "his brothers hated him for his dreams and his words." When God inspires you with a big idea, you will sometimes be prosecuted for it when you share that idea with friends and relatives. You may be discouraged and even hated because of what you shared. The key is to remain focus on your goals and concentrate on the end achievement of that plan that is a promise that would come to pass, if you do not lose focus.

In Genesis 37: 23-28 "So when Joseph came to his brothers, they stripped him of his robe--- the richly ornamented robe he was wearing and they took him and threw him into the cistern; an empty pit;" and later it was recorded that he was sold to the Ishmaelite's for money. Because Joseph had a dream, he was hated, but even when he was thrown into a pit, it was recorded that he was not overwhelmed by sadness, fear or doubts. His condition in a dry hole could not derail him because his focus was on his dreams not on the condition he was in.

Sometimes you see people who are happy, although there is nothing to be happy about on the outside. This is because they have a dream which is known to them alone. Certain difficult circumstances would try to pull you away from your dreams and cause you to look at the externals or your problems, and thereby cause you to forget your dreams. We do not look at what is seen, but what is unseen, for what is seen is temporary while what is unseen is permanent. As children of God, we walk by faith, not by sight. We, therefore, are not overwhelmed by what is seen.

As it was stated in the Bible, after Joseph was sold, he was favored by the King of that region, but later on, he was thrown in jail because he refused Potiphar's wife's advances to sleep with her. He did not allow the prison condition to overwhelm him.

Instead he looked through the window, saw the beautiful skies and gave thanks to God. He knew he did not belong in the prison, but a much better place. He thought so because of the dreams God had put in his mind and he had felt. He had a dream that someday even the stars would bow to him. (Genesis 37:9). What is your dream? How big is it? Does it give you joy on the inside when you think of it? If it does, know that this is the dream God has planted in your mind that would come true if you focus on it. Each time you find yourself doubting the promises God put in your mind, refocus on your dreams that are in your mind.

Tell yourself that the future you have is better than your present circumstance. Say to yourself these words when you feel as if things are not going your way.

"My words must be the portrait of the future I have in my mind and the hope God has given me."

"My action, my behavior, my way of life and everything about me must be the portrait of the future I want. When I find myself in the place or circumstances which are contrary to the image I have in mind, I must remember to say to myself, "I know where I belong- not here in these circumstances. This is only temporary; this is only for a short time. I will get out of this. When I speak and think as such, this will impart in me the strength to persevere and will help me overcome the situation that I find myself in."

If you are a man or woman of vision, you will be able to know where you belong. When Joseph was in the pit, he knew the condition there was for a short time. I am sure he was thinking, this is not where I belong, this is not the promise of God for my life. I have a greater promise than this. Now that I know where I belong, I will not complain about my circumstances anymore. I will not worry what people have to say about me.

I will not have to beg or cry that I am overwhelmed by the challenges of life that I found myself in because they are only temporary. The condition and difficulties shall pass and the promise that God has placed in my mind will come to pass. My dreams will be fulfilled because they are guaranteed by God. Joseph knew where he belonged, that it was not in the pit.

He knew he would not die in the pit. He knew he would live to see the glory of God. His dreams came to pass. Remember, our troubles become easier to handle when we know that they will not last. When God puts something in your mind, the circumstances, what people say or what happens around you, cannot change the mind if you do not let it. Remember, it was what God put in Joseph's mind that was his focus when he was in the dry pit, in the prison yard and in Potiphar's house. When you face a challenge, remember this, sometimes God uses such problem to bring us to himself so that we can draw strength from his word, his power and position ourselves to possess what he has placed in our mind.

At the time Joseph had the dreams of his future, he was too young to appreciate the glory that were ahead of him. So the difficulties he faced along the way were to prepare him for the inevitable success ahead. If Joseph had not been in prison, he would not have had the contact that finally linked him to the royal throne of Egypt, and he would not have gained the insight needed to be a ruler.

Sometimes hard times are tools that God uses to equip us for the coming task ahead. Also, it is by ways of difficult challenges that we come in contact with people that will help us achieve our goals. Change your thoughts and don't let your words of doom and failure defeat you in life. Set a watch on your mouth and stop those doubt-filled, negative words. They do not agree with God's promises for your life. When things look bad, and you are believing in promises of financial blessings, it's better to keep your mouth shut than to go around "poor mouthing yourself," telling everyone your financial woes.

I have learned that when you speak negatively of your finances, you dig yourself a hole so deep that it becomes a challenge to get out. But if you take the time to program your heart by saying what God says about your financial situation, you can have victory over apparent economic defeat.

As Jesus answered them in Mathew 21:21, "Truly I tell you, if you have faith and do not doubt, not only can you do what was done to the fig tree, but also you can say to the mountain, 'Go, throw yourself into the sea,' and it will be done."

"But shall believe that those things which he say shall come to pass; he shall have whatever he say." Mark 11:23

WHAT IS YOUR CALLING

What do you want to do? What is it that you can do? What is the one thing that when you do it, it will give you the ultimate joy when it becomes a reality in your life, and perhaps will also give others the pleasure and satisfaction of life through that act? Your dream can materialize when you believe in the essence of its reality. What is your dream? If your dream is to go back to college to be a plumber, an electrician, a singer, an artist, a lawyer, a teacher, or a doctor, anything you want. What you want to become will come true when you work and begin to take the necessary steps to accomplish its truth.

Whatever it is that you've always wanted to be, you can be that person when you act according to your heart's instructions. Remember, you are like a channel through which God's blessings flow to people. Without you, God cannot do his good will which he designed to come through you. You are a service onto men from God.

All the dreams or ideas you have can be fulfilled when you take the initiative to act on them and live them. When you doubt your ability to do what your mind has conceived, you slowly put to death the potential of that idea or your dream becoming what it was intended to be. And, as you continue to doubt your ability or the life force in that thought, the image gradually fades away.

The ideas faded away because of several factors: (1) You doubted its potentiality, and (2); you underestimated your power as a child of God to do what is already true in you. (3); you invalidated your real worth. Remember that each time you doubt your ability to do anything, you have diminished your chance of new revelation or knowledge.

In Ephesians 5:13-14, Paul wrote about the manifestation of the word that has been conceived and made possible by the light. Light symbolizes knowledge or intelligence, therefore, when you imagine an idea (good idea), act on it because it is meant to be revealed and manifested. Every good idea you conceive is knowledge waiting to be shared. You cannot share knowledge when it's hidden amidst the cloud of self-doubt and fear.

Every idea has life, power and authority inherent in it to bring it to pass. Your dreams can awaken when you activate the life force in it, by believing in the essence of its reality and doing according to what is required to fulfill that dream.

In the Bible, Lazarus the brother of Mary, was a clear illustration of how dead dreams or ideas can come to life or are raised up from the tomb when its truth is believed. In the book of John, 11:1-27, Lazarus was presumed dead by his family members until Christ was called to do something. Christ went to the tomb where Lazarus was laid and asked for the stone to be moved.

In fact, they told Christ that he had been dead for four days, and the stench from Lazarus body was evident that he had been dead for a long time. Christ told the multitudes that he was not dead, but only sleeping. Christ commanded him to rise up and walk, and he did. This biblical illustration parallels your buried dreams and ideas.

Your dreams are not fulfilled either because you doubt the possibility or by the negative criticism you got from others when you shared your ideas. You may have doubt it in your heart because you do not see how the dream you have could come through for you. In Luke Chapter 1 vs. 1- 52, the Angel Gabriel appeared to Zachariah and told him that his dream has been answered and told him that God sent him to give him, Zachariah the good news; that his wife Elizabeth would bear him a son. Zachariah was doubtful and said to the angel; how can this be? I am old, and my wife is well advanced in age, and I, I am an old man. My wife, he continues is barren; how can she bear me a son? The angel had to shut his mouth before he spoiled his blessings.

The dreams and thoughts you have of yourself as someone special or to have an invention that would benefit you and benefit others is prophesied from God. The angels are the thoughts that this can happen if you work towards it and believe its manifestation. Sometimes you don't even need to do anything because the concept of it alone in your mind is strong enough to compel the manifestation of a dream to reality.

If you read the verse that I mentioned, you will see that Zachariah's dreams and prayers for a child was fulfilled and his wife Elizabeth had a son and named him John; the name the Angel Gabriel instructed him to call the child. When you doubt your dreams, it weakens you spiritually. The residual effects of your doubting thoughts produced a weakened self that could not do anything about your dreams.

In regards to Lazarus dying, the symbol of the stench is somewhat similar to the lethargic feelings that weigh you down and sometimes makes you feel powerless and unable to do anything for yourself. It can also be seen as a sense of being sick or near death. When the power of knowledge comes and shines a light in your mind, you are awakened to believe in the truth of who you are again. If you recall each time you conceived a good idea in your mind; you will come to life as you begin to see its possibility in your mind's eye.

Every instance that you negate the reality of an idea, you are stunting its growth in you or the revelation of knowledge that was supposed to take place. Ideas on their own are nothing when you don't act on them. A good idea if not acted upon produces terrible psychological pain. An idea has value when you work on it. Acting on your ideas will produce mental tranquility and satisfaction of accomplishment. Christ is like the truth of your dreams and until you call forth the truth of your dreams for a better life, it lays dormant like the dead Lazarus.

When you believe in the goodness of the ideas you have, the truth in it will give you confidence and boldness to do what is right. The life force in any idea, when believed, will compel you to gain insight and confidence in carrying out the plan. Any dream or idea you have conceived can be accomplished. Every man was called to represent and honor the image that formed him.

Man is a representation of God's image that is good. Man is referred to as an inventor and is called to believe in what is always good. But many don't stand the chance of fulfilling their destiny because of the false confession that comes out of their mouth daily. You can change your thinking by reading this book repeatedly and taking action. You can start this change when you begin to see yourself living above the squalor, pain and sadness that you are in, and in time opportunity will present itself for you to move out of the environment that has kept you bound. The good is always around and within you.

If you do not see a change, don't worry, your dreams for what you wish for will come to pass when you don't lose hope. If the change you want, or the things you wish to manifest did not come as quickly as you think it should, the reason might be the way you're thinking of it. Re-examine your thoughts again and think about what it is you want to change. Sometimes what we want at the time we want it may conflict with the real intention of wanting that thing. If your plans are aligned right, there is always a time period for everything to happen.

If your dream is delayed, don't lose hope or focus, continue to see it happening and it will come to pass. If it didn't happen, it's because we gave up on the dream happening. If you are in a situation that you wish to get out of, believe in the truth of envisioning yourself getting out of your predicament. If you are hoping on falling in love, it will not fail you. If you want something and it is a plan that needs action, by taking steps in accomplishing that which you have envisioned, the truth of the idea you are aiming at will bring about ways and insight that will guide you in achieving that plan. Remember no man is a passing stream, every man is born unique with his own special talent and purpose; so activate your ability and use by believing in the Christ in you.

Sometimes many people see life like a man I call Mr. Adamu, a young man that came to the United States to visit his best friend. Mr. Adamu is from the Northern part of the Sahara in Western Africa. He was used to walking miles in the desert and was not familiar to high-rise buildings. So to see his friend who lives on the 30th floor of a high-rise complex in a metropolitan city in the USA, Adamu did what came naturally. He proceeded to use the staircase, not knowing there was an elevator that could take him to the 30th floor.

While on the 20th floor, a young man opened the stair door and saw Adamu breathing heavily in exhaustion from climbing the stairs. The man asked Adamu if he was okay and he responded to the man that he was going up and didn't understand why they had such tall houses as this, and staircases that were difficult to climb.

The young man looked at Adamu and asked him what floor he was going to? "The 30th floor," Adamu responded. The young man chuckled and said to Adamu. "The elevator is right there," as he pointed to the exit sign that led to an elevator that could take him to the 30th floor in seconds. Hearing this, Adamu was taken aback that he had spent several minutes climbing the staircase to the 20ᵗʰfloor while there was an elevator that could have taken a lot faster.

Although there is nothing wrong with taking the stairs, many of us go through life like Mr. Adamu, not knowing the abundance of blessings around us. This is because we are so used to the old ways of doing things that sometimes we don't see any other way. We believe the hard way is the best when in actuality, hardship doesn't often equate to efficiency.

The truth is; if we look a little further, think a little deeper, believe a little stronger in our ability to see the good for ourselves we will get an answer to our most complex questions. But many people can't imagine themselves living above what they are used to. So even when new ideas are revealed to them, they cannot see beyond what they already know because of the old way of thinking and seeing things.

Adamu had absolutely no idea that there was an elevator to take him to where he was going. He knew only of the old way of doing things, climbing and walking long miles to wherever he wanted to go. This is not to say that walking up the stairs is a wrong thing. It was just not efficient at that moment. The truth is always available to us, but many of us are sometimes so clouded by the old ways of seeing things that even when we confront new ideas, we sometimes lack the courage to do things differently. The truth will always reveal itself to those who are receptive and want to get what they wish to see.

Luckily for Adamu in his quest to ask why a house should be built so tall, he inadvertently revealed what he wanted to know, which is, how to get to the apartment he was going to quickly. The elevator could do that for him. The innate good will always lead us to say and do what it is we want to do or know when we are receptive to it.

DO WHAT IS RIGHT

❖❖❖❖❖❖

Mental efficiency is contingent upon harmony. Discord means confusion, and, therefore, he who acquires love must be in harmony with God. When we think correctly, and when we understand the truth centered deep in our soul, the thought sent through our body is constructive; hence the sensations will be pleasant and harmonious. The result of thinking correctly is that we build strength, vitality, and all constructive forces into our body. It is also through this same mind that all distress, sickness, lack, limitation and every form of discord is allowed into our lives that weaken us. It is then through our mind, by wrong thinking, that we are connected to all destructive forces.

Some people have wondered why they are not reaping prosperity when they've been doing the right thing all their life. My advice and question are for you to check your life. Every time you think you failed or might have failed in doing something you wished to do; re-evaluate that situation, you would rightly discern that your thoughts, actions or lack of actions led to that failure. You were either afraid that you would lose or you allowed fearful and doubtful thoughts into your mind that provoked a reaction to your failure. But be not discouraged because failing in doing or accomplishing something is a chance to start again.

As Socrates would say: "The unexamined life is not worth living." I Implore you to re-examine your past, your life, and see what you could have done differently or even better and do it, and make another plan to transform and reinvent yourself. What is it that you are doing? If you think you have been doing the right things and nothing seems to happen, I would ask you to examine your life again and start anew. And, if you are among those who have perhaps thought this way, may I suggest that you start a mental purging of your mind and heart of all the thoughts of ill will or anger of the past. If you think you have wronged people in the past or think people have hurt you, forgive them all and forgive your self.

This way forward for you is that you can start with a clean slate. Also, if you've been lying, stealing, cheating, bearing false witness and doing things you know in your heart are wrong, begin today to remove those thoughts from your mind and heart. Repent of them and do them no more. See yourself living in the reality of what is true from all the circumstances you have cleansed from your mind. Think of your mind as a garden, filled with various plants like flowers and weeds. Each flower or plant represents what you have planted in the past. And your heart represents the ground or soil where all these flowers and plants have taken root to grow.

Take the weeds out and leave the flowers that you want to keep. Your mind will tell you how you want the garden to look. It is through your mind that you will see the garden the way you want it to be. And each flower represents your thoughts or what you have been sowing all along. When you cleanse your mind, the garden, visualize again what plant you want to sow into it.

So begin now to plant the type of flowers you would like to see or have around. Be prepared to guard your garden always because some plants like weeds will grow out of the ones you've planted to stunt their growth. Be prepared to uproot the plant you do not want in the garden because each plant or flower (which is the symbolic representation of your thoughts), will take root in the soil and grow. Your heart and mind have to be in accordance with each other, if they disagree, the seed will not grow. The blueprint in your mind has to match what your heart is feeling.

The emotions in your heart and the thoughts in your mind have to be in union with the picture and growth of the image you have. Your mind works 24/7, and other thoughts will always come up to tell you that the seed, the flower you are planting is ugly and couldn't possibly be right. You must resist those thoughts because they are not for the growth of your seed, instead continue to believe in the value of what you have seeded. Faith is the evidence of things hoped for, the vision you have will come true when you hold onto it long enough.

Whatever image you conceive in your mind and believe in your heart will be for you as you've conceived it. There is power in the seed, which is your thought. Thoughts are a powerful force, and when nourished with deep emotions, will manifest as the picture you had in mind. I will tell you a short story about the power of the mind and how I discovered that it could be work against us when not used correctly.

Several years ago I was in Western Europe for a Study Abroad Program, and while there I visited a friend who invited me to his family home. I wanted to take a photograph of him and his girlfriend and other people. I was excited about taking the picture. I had already asked that the photo be taken, but then, I had a change of heart and didn't want the picture taken anymore because of how I felt about this young man. The feelings I had for his girlfriend were neither of love nor of hate, but a neutral feeling of calmness and nothingness.

So, I thought to myself what is the point of taking this picture when I know how I'll feel when I see myself with this man and his girlfriend in the photo? So I silently said in my head, "I don't want any picture of my friend and his girl and me to emerge in print." The picture was taken and then another.

I returned to the United States and went to the nearest pharmacy store to develop the negatives, and guess what? The exact picture that I didn't want to be taken with the pal and his girlfriend never developed. There was no image in the space where it was supposed to be. That is, not even an image or shadow of someone expressed itself in the negative, but black space. The shots that were taken before and after the picture I didn't want had prints of images. What this apparently told me was never to do that again, never to wish for something you may later regret, because the mind is a powerful weapon.

I have learned and I'm still learning to accept what comes to me at a particular moment by only changing my feeling or response towards that event or environment because that's where the power lies. The answer given to a circumstance is what defines the moment. I also realized that I had the power within me to make things happen. And what I prompt to happen should be what blesses and edifies others and myself.

The power of our subconscious mind will always do what we impress upon it. My plea to you is, don't use it for evil.

Interestingly, there are so many people who use this power to perpetuate cruelty and to poison the minds of those perceived to be weak and unaware of the tremendous power within them. The power within you is meant only for good, for you and others. If I had allowed the picture taken with positive thoughts, I would have relished in showing it to others and perhaps having fond memories of it years later when I see it. What this experience also taught me is this, I may have gotten my wish and I can always take another picture with the same person, but that moment in which it happened may never be recaptured.

Though I could try to replicate the scene of the event by going back to Europe, visiting the same place and asking the same people to take another picture with me, it may never be the same. Scenes and events can be recreated, but when a life decision choice is altered, it may never be reversed or recreated. So why am I sharing this experience with you? I am sharing this experiences because I have experienced that although thoughts may seem like a simple thing; it is through thoughts that great things come to pass.

Our thoughts are powerful though very benign and, as a matter of fact, considered as nothing by those who don't know its power, but they are none-the-less, the instrument we use to make things happen around us, consciously and unconsciously for us and for others.

Our thoughts like swords can be a dangerous weapon to cut ourselves and hurt others when we don't use them correctly. Your heart, the soil is always fertile, and the seat on which your mind rests is alive and does as it is instructed. But don't be fooled, what one sows, that also shall the person reap. Sow good thoughts and reap good thoughts. Sow evil thoughts, you receive evil actions. I didn't get the picture that I didn't want, but by that lesson I now know the real meaning of what the Lord said in the Bible, "Vengeance is mine, leave it unto me," because it is really for our own good.

When we do things to hurt others even without knowing, we are not living according to the righteousness of the good within us. At the same time even when we are aware of the righteousness within us, we are not to condemn ourselves. In all things, we are meant to live righteously on this earth.

The life force of soil and seeds are in accordance with reality. The power of your mind and thoughts are also principled, that is, the way they were meant to work. There is life latent in the seed. Whatever seed you plant in the soil will grow. Therefore, resist the weeds that want to overtake the real fruit. When I mean resist, I mean to change the thoughts that are not in harmony with the goodness of your heart. Change it by focusing only on ideas that are beautiful, don't let the weeds grow and spread; weeds in this sense are negative feelings or thoughts.

Each weed planted will keep growing as long as the soil is fertile. When you believe for your good, and the good of others, resist accepting what is not true of that good idea.

As a matter of fact, stay away from the path that you know will lead you to believe or act out what is false. Entertain good thoughts in your heart and begin to see your dreams become real. Believe in the truth of your dreams and don't ever doubt its reality, because it will come to pass.

Plant the seed that will grow and produce fruits that people can eat and enjoy. Let your ideas be the dreams that involve other people's well-being, and you too will benefit from it. The simple truth is that life is about decisions.

Every decision you've made in the past through your thoughts has determined for you what your experience is today. As Apostle Paul said in the book of Philippians 4:8.

"Finally, brothers and sisters, whatever is true, whatever is noble, whatever is right, whatever is pure, whatever is lovely, whatever is admirable—if anything is excellent or praiseworthy—think about such things."

If you have visualized your garden, your mind, as clean, you are a new person. Therefore, begin today to sow the seed of virtue, which is, whatever is lovely and true of you and others. Your dream about what you want to do is your service to the world. Activate your dreams by doing what is right to accomplish them. Start now and do not wait, and the life of Christ that is already in you will continue to guide and encourage you always to do what is good.

CREATE THE LIFE YOU WANT

Life is a decision; life is about love. You choose the kind of beautiful life you want to live and focus on the good you want to be and on how to achieve that goal, or else, you will be bouncing back and forth.

Loving the self that wants life is of the essence to being; because all you are is love personified and being aware that you are love; is powerful. Love moves the world and you are part of that love that moves the world. You are a thinking person, you are creative and you are moving forward. We grow every day as we breathe in life. I am still growing because there is so much more to this beautiful life that I can think of.

You can look at life as two parallel lines. The life of God, the love, the creative energy which is and always has been with you; the pure essence that created you and dwells in you. The life of God will continue to be in you until you physically leave this earth when it is your time. And then, there is the life that is in this world; the world system that is created by man.

These two lines can be said to be in one single path, but very different. The life of God is in the city of God, and the life of the world is in the Adamic man, the self-life, controlled by all the existence of the worldly thought system.

The life of God is in the life of Christ, the truth of who you are if you believe in Christ. So now the question is as a child of the Almighty God, the son of the creator of heaven and earth who has already bestowed upon you all that you need to live life abundantly: What city do you want to dwell in? You have to choose which city to live in. In the city of God where all that you need resides or in the self-centered man, the self that is controlled by the world thought system that passes away. Unfortunately, many of us came into this world by and through the force of the unbelieving man; wrong thinking.

We are now farther away from the right understanding of our relation to God. But a person who is far away from what is truthful can also draw close to God when the word of truth is awakened again. How can the truth be awakened in a person who is not aware of the real presence of God within him? By desiring and believing that the Lord Jesus Christ is the Lord and Savior of his life; that is the truth he should think on. And when he does seek and believe such, he shall find, because he who asks, will receive and he who seeks shall find, especially if what he seeks is what is already given.

The life of God is real freedom and is within all man. Unless one knows this truth personally, the person will be wondering from one part of the world to another looking for the peace that is always within him. So now, we come down to the decisions we make to create change, if change is what we want.

If you are such a person and you are living this life without hope of change or the knowledge of the riches, blessings and love that is within you, what should you do? Are you going to continue with the lack of knowledge or choose the path of knowledge concerning the truth within you? To create the life you will love, you have to let the Christ in you lead and help you create this new life.

The truth is forever present with you and calling you to draw closer and gaze towards it alone. Through this way, things will begin to fall into place calmly as the gentle wave of the sea. Your duty will be to trust it and continuously obey His tender, but forever audible loving voice saying, "all is well to him that enters into the glory of God." Do right, love God, yourself and family and make a genuine effort to do good for others by reaching out to those in need, irrelevant if they are part of your family or friends. Do the right thing, and love and be kind to yourself and to your neighbors.

The self that is suffering will fall away, and in its place the new you, which was already there before you were ever conceived and brought into this world, it will emerge and remain. "For as a man thinketh in his heart, so is he." Psalm 23:7.

MOTIVATION FOR WRITING THE BOOK

❖❖❖❖❖❖

One of the motivations for this book "Life Is About Decision, Life is About Love," is the result of the experience that was spurned by my decision, though unconsciously driven to leave a job I had. Several years ago when I was working as a flight attendant with a major American airlines' regional carrier and towards the end of my employment with the airline, I was assigned the Reserve Line. A Reserve Line is when you are assigned a standby status and can only work when you are assigned a flight. The flight could be given to you one day in advance or as little as two hours in advance.

I had thought that working the Reserve Line would help me manage my work and still go to school; since that was the main reason I was in the United States. But my choosing the Reserve line that month was nothing but a huge mistake. I could barely pay my bills and was not enjoying school and I was very upset with myself for making such a miserable mistake. The best idea I could come up with at that time given that I really wanted to focus on school, was to leave the job so that I could concentrate in school; this was a conscious thought in my mind. What a brilliant idea, right? As the law goes, sometimes what you focus on with an intense desire comes to pass in swift motion even if it was for a second. Within days, I had given up my job in a manner that was not entirely pleasing.

It happened because I had accepted the decision to leave the job in my mind and unconsciously I sabotaged my effort from working in that company. The unconscious steps began one morning when I was driving to work. I had left home in time to get a parking space close to the airport in order to ride the train to the airport from the parking garage. For some strange reason, I could not find a parking space for an entire hour and a half.

I drove around several times in the neighborhood where I would take the train to the airport and could not find a parking space. The time to report to work came and went and I was still looking for a parking space. Finally, I found a space to park my car and ran to the train station to the nearest pay phone and called the scheduling department. I told the scheduler that I could not find a parking space. That was not their problem. I was supposed to sign in at 6.45 a.m. for my 7.45 a.m. Flight and I did not. I eventually made it to the airport at 7.15 a.m and ran to the aircraft in the hopes of catching the briefing, but the aircraft was not in its usual spot. I thought the flight had departed, so I ran to the flight control room and checked the computer screen and saw that my flight was delayed due to an inbound aircraft that had not arrived. I blew a sigh of relief because at last I would make my flight. I went to my manager and told her what happened that morning. I informed her that I was late in signing in.

I apologized for being late, but she was indifferent and insisted on giving me a "No Show," although I was standing in front of her. She was not empathetic to my situation. She told me that I did not call the scheduler to report for my flight and as such, she was taking me out of the entire trip.

"What I thought to myself." She had no reason to place me on a "No Show," when I was at the airport and had explained my situation to her and had honestly called into the crew scheduler to report the situation. She insisted on putting me on a "No Show," so I told her that if she gives me a "No Show" which is like making me absent, I would go home. She said, "You couldn't do that." Well, I did just that. I left her office and went home and slept. But few days later, I was asked to see the manager in her office for a meeting with the other departmental administrators. My flight manager had reported me.

The situation was handled unfairly and the manner I was treated was like a criminal when, in fact, what happened to me could easily have happened to anyone. I felt their behavior to me was racially prejudiced, so I went and filed for an unemployment benefit after they terminated my employment. But the company opposed it, insisting that I quit the job and should not get unemployment. I did not quit the job so I fought back and insisted on getting my insurance claim because of what happened that morning was unintentional. I felt I was provoked by my manager to leave the job and go home. The fact was; they fired me unlawfully.

I got the insurance benefit after the unemployment panel judge ruled that I was wrongfully dismissed. I was able to get unemployment benefit and then I went back to school full-time, but I was not happy with that decision. Yeah, maybe I got what I wanted. I was in school full-time and receiving some financial benefit, but later on I realized that there were other options that would have allowed me to keep my job and still go to school. First, I should not have bid for the Reserve Line if I was not willing to commit wholeheartedly to the Reserve Line. I should have bid scheduled flight lines and then ask my colleagues to exchange flights for off days with me. I could also have dropped some flights and lose money so I could go to school. There were other options available, but I never saw them or sought to know those options. The fact is, our thinking creates events that cause things to happen in our lives. And whether we believe it or not, it does.

It was after this experience that I realized how my thinking prior to losing my job activated the events that led to the loss of my job. It was also during this period that I understood the importance of my thoughts and that life is about decisions. Right after my ordeal I began to understand the process that led to my job loss that I had created that pattern with the way I was thinking about the situation. Decisions, though subtle, can create a domino effect that take you further away from your first intention. We create almost everything that happens to us through our thoughts which lead to our decisions.

On a side note: The manager that encouraged my termination from one of the best first jobs I have held as a student in the United States had also gotten what she sowed. I was told by a former roommate that few months after I lost the job, she got fired from her managerial position with the airline for being late. The very thing she accused me of.

The other motivation for this book came about as a result of the way I had felt about life at a particular time. I was tired of life and had gone to bed thinking about just leaving this earth. That night I had a dream and saw my father who had passed away several months earlier. My dad died tragically, and I had been very distraught because the last time I saw my dad was ten years before he died.

I never saw him again, although I had spoken to him several times over the phone. I was in pain, depressed and I felt entirely hopeless because I missed my father and wished he were still alive. So in my dream I honestly wanted to know what I should do with my life, as I was hopelessly sad and distraught. I was also experiencing suicidal thoughts and could not find help from anyone that I knew. In that dream, my father told me something that is also part of the motivating factors in writing this book; that Life Is About Love.

I asked my dad what I should do to be happy. I remember seeing him seated in a white leather chair in my studio apartment in Chicago, as the personification of God. In that dream, he personified purity to the highest degree, and I knew after I woke up that morning that my father was in a very peaceful and heavenly place. When I asked my dad what I should do to be happy, he told me these simple words.

"Everything you want my child, you have. You want a dress, you have it; you want a car, you have it. Whatever it is that you wished for, you have. It meant that, if what I wanted were peace and love, then it was mine. The answer my father gave to the question that I asked him in the dream was very disappointing. I was hoping that he would give me a magic formula in the dream so that when I woke up I could use it to make my life a better and happier one. But, in fact, years later, I realized that he gave me more than a magic formula.

My father told me the gospel truth; the word of God. Everything I ever wanted, I have because it has freely been given to me. I honestly did not understand it in that dream or even when I woke up. I had always dreamt of coming to United States of America and schooling and I was in the United States and had completed my university education at the University of Illinois. How did that happen?

I wrote this book with the inspiration to inspire and to heal myself from the pain of loss that I felt after my father passed and also to encourage others who are in similar circumstances. During my experiences, I felt like my spiritual journey was interrupted when I allowed the pressure from the outside world to creep into my mind. I realized a blessed life doing what I loved. I had traveled extensively as a flight attendant working with major international airlines. I visited and stayed in many African, European countries and many States and cities in the United States and had spectacular experiences. I met so many people that have enriched my life; so what else but to be thankful.

I wanted healing and I had it. If I needed money, I had it. But I did not realize then that the energy to get anything in this life originated from God and within me. The gospel truth is that everything we ever wanted, we already have it. Peace, life and everything you can think of God already gave it.

Isn't it factual that if I wanted a dress that I would get it? I wanted to write a book, and I did. I wanted a car and to drive, and I did. I had a car, how did I get it? It was not instantaneous, but I did get a car when I wanted one. All you have to do is see what it is you want and believe you have it. The details of how to get what you need will come to you. My father was right, and so is God the Creator of our soul, the giver of the Spirit life in us.

WHY THE NAME GOD

I used the name God and Jesus Christ as a representation of the essence I felt. For me, there is no other name universally understood as worthy that I can use to call the Joy that I felt while writing this book or the truth of what it is I am talking about. I could have chosen to use the word principle to describe the force that compelled me to write. But I prefer the word God because it is what many have known to be the name that represents the power of life that brought us into this world. The truth of God, Jesus Christ, are the spirit and peace that is within us all.

If any man should say that there is no God, or a reality within him that is the same as in all man on earth, it means that the person speaking is not living. Therefore, to claim that there is no God is to say there is no life, no air, and no living things. Therefore, to think correctly is to know that God does exist.

It is a lie to believe that there is no principle within a man that is all right and real.

The truth is when we are confronted with life-altering predicament; we often call on this invisible force to save us.

And often when a person believes with assurance, he is saved because this power is always life-ward and responds to a call towards goodness and growth. So, if, at a perceived doom one may call on this invisible power to save him; why not reverence and worship that invisible presence. I will say to everyone reading this book to recognize the hidden spirit that is visible in times of joy and good health. Because the unseen name which some may refuse to accept as God is the life in them. And if there is life in man, then that life in him is created by the name that created heaven and earth. Call him whatever name you choose, but as a Christian, I call him Christ, Jesus, and God.

THE END

AUTHOR'S NOTE

❖❖❖❖❖❖

Some of the words used in writing this book are repetitive and may seem almost childlike in manner. The words were used deliberately and in order to reaffirm the truth that the process of the thought system is also repetitive and natural. The only difference lies in what is being thought of, because the process of the thought system is the same. Like the illustration of the seed time and harvest time in the Bible. You plant a seed; you water it, and it grows. It is the same process, no matter what seed is being planted.

ACKNOWLEDGEMENTS

While it may seem that the vision and inspiration for writing this book came to me to write it, the manifestation of this book would not have been, if not for the people who aided me along the way. I thank you all and you know who you are.

Thanks to God, the giver of life, power and strength without which I could not have written this book. I want to thank my dear Nathan A, who also inspired me by his love and faith in me to be a loving mother to him; I pray for the best that life in God would give him. Thanks to my family, and to the memory of my father who motivated me to write this book. Thanks, Yaya.

AUTHOR'S PROFILE

❖❖❖❖❖❖

Blessing Bess Otobo was born in Nigeria. Ms. Otobo studied at the University of Illinois in Chicago and has a B.A in Creative Writing and English, and M.A in Psychology from National-Louis University Chicago. She has two other published books and is currently working on other fiction and non-fiction narratives. Ms. Otobo lives in the USA.

No part of this book may be used or reproduced by any means, graphic, electronic or mechanic without the written permission of the author. Permission to use any portion of this book should be sent via email to the author @ botobo1@yahoo.com or by sending her email via her Facebook or Twitter account below.

https://www.facebook.com/bess.jeanty

https://twitter.com/BOTOBO1

botobo1@yahoo.com

Printed in Great Britain
by Amazon

82622091R00078